THE UPPER ROOM

WHERE THE WORLD MEETS TO PRAY

Daniele Och
UK editor

INVITATIONAL
INTERDENOMINATIONAL
INTERNATIONAL

36 LANGUAGES
Multiple formats are available in some languages

15 The Chambers, Vineyard
Abingdon OX14 3FE
brf.org.uk

Bible Reading Fellowship (BRF) is a charity (233280)
and company limited by guarantee (301324),
registered in England and Wales

ISBN 978 1 80039 188 8
All rights reserved

Originally published in the USA by The Upper Room® upperroom.org
US edition © 2023 The Upper Room, Nashville, TN (USA). All rights reserved.
This edition © Bible Reading Fellowship 2023
Cover photo by Jess Bailey Designs

Acknowledgements

Scripture quotations marked with the following abbreviations are taken from the
version shown. Where no abbreviation is given, the quotation is taken from the same
version as the headline reference.

NIV: The Holy Bible, New International Version (Anglicised edition) copyright © 1979,
1984, 2011 by Biblica. Used by permission of Hodder & Stoughton Publishers, an
Hachette UK company. All rights reserved. 'NIV' is a registered trademark of Biblica.
UK trademark number 1448790.

NRSV: The New Revised Standard Version Updated Edition. Copyright © 2021
National Council of the Churches of Christ in the United States of America. Used by
permission. All rights reserved worldwide.

CEB: copyright © 2011 by Common English Bible.

KJV: the Authorised Version of the Bible (The King James Bible), the rights in which
are vested in the Crown, are reproduced by permission of the Crown's Patentee,
Cambridge University Press.

A catalogue record for this book is available from the British Library

Printed by Gutenberg Press, Tarxien, Malta

How to use *The Upper Room*

The Upper Room is ideal in helping us spend a quiet time with God each day. Each daily entry is based on a passage of scripture and is followed by a meditation and prayer. Each person who contributes a meditation to the magazine seeks to relate their experience of God in a way that will help those who use *The Upper Room* every day.

Here are some guidelines to help you make best use of *The Upper Room*:

1 Read the passage of scripture. It is a good idea to read it more than once, in order to have a fuller understanding of what it is about and what you can learn from it.
2 Read the meditation. How does it relate to your own experience? Can you identify with what the writer has outlined from their own experience or understanding?
3 Pray the written prayer. Think about how you can use it to relate to people you know or situations that need your prayers today.
4 Think about the contributor who has written the meditation. Some users of *The Upper Room* include this person in their prayers for the day.
5 Meditate on the 'Thought for the day' and the 'Prayer focus', perhaps using them again as the focus for prayer or direction for action.

Why is it important to have a daily quiet time? Many people will agree that it is the best way of keeping in touch every day with the God who sustains us and who sends us out to do his will and show his love to the people we encounter each day. Meeting with God in this way reassures us of his presence with us, helps us to discern his will for us and makes us part of his worldwide family of Christian people through our prayers.

I hope that you will be encouraged as you use the magazine regularly as part of your daily devotions, and that God will richly bless you as you read his word and seek to learn more about him.

Daniele Och
UK editor

Helping to pay it forward

Living Faith... resourcing your spiritual journey

As part of our Living Faith ministry, we're raising funds to give away copies of Bible reading notes and other resources to those who aren't able to access them any other way, working with food banks and chaplaincy services, in prisons, hospitals and care homes.
If you've enjoyed and benefited from our resources, would you consider paying it forward to enable others to do so too?

Make a gift at **brf.org.uk/donate**

Crossing the Jordan

[Jesus] went away again across the Jordan to the place where John had been baptising earlier, and he remained there. Many came to him, and they were saying, 'John performed no sign, but everything that John said about this man was true.' And many believed in him there.
John 10:40–42 (NRSV)

In this scripture passage, the apostle John records a detail that is often overlooked. As Jesus makes his final journey towards Jerusalem, John says that Jesus crosses the Jordan river at the place where John the Baptiser had met him a few years earlier. Jesus' wading through the Jordan and crossing into more Romanised territories – instead of playing it safe and sojourning among his Jewish compatriots – crystallises the global, intercessory mission of the people of Israel, Jesus and the church.

Throughout the Bible, crossing through water symbolises the birth of something new: a new covenant people (Exodus 14:21–25; Joshua 3), a new advent of God (Mark 1:9–10), and now a renewed mission to 'go into all the world and proclaim the good news' (Mark 16:15), and not just to those who look, think and act like us. John Wesley, one of the founders of the Methodist movement, paraphrased this call with the words, 'The world is my parish.'

As we move into the heart of 2023, will we have the holy courage to wade into the depths of God's love and grace, and follow Jesus 'across the Jordan'? Let us remember our baptism and renew our commitment to our global gospel mission.

Revd Kimberly Orr
World editor and publisher

Spanish edition

Writers featured in this issue of *The Upper Room*:

• Julianis Báez Pichardo (Dominican Republic)
• Ruth Mancilla (Mexico)
• Sandra dos Santos (Uruguay)

Gifts to the international editions of
The Upper Room help the world meet to pray.
upperroom.org/gift

The editor writes...

'What do you have against me, man of God? Did you come to remind me of my sin and kill my son?'
1 Kings 17:18 (NIV)

The story of the widow at Zarephath is not the best known of the episodes in Elijah's dramatic life, as told in 1 Kings. But for me it reveals as much about both the awe-inspiring power and the tender-hearted grace of God as the two more familiar stories that follow it (the contest with the prophets of Baal on Mount Carmel, and the Lord's 'still, small voice' at Horeb).

While famine ravages the land, the prophet Elijah is led to the home of a widow and her son who face starvation. In a demonstration of his sovereign power, however, God causes the widow's supply of food to miraculously never run out until the famine is over. So far, so good.

But then the boy falls ill and the widow watches on helpless as his condition deteriorates, until finally he dies. The woman, distraught, lashes out at Elijah, in the verse quoted above. She has seen that his God is powerful, but that doesn't mean that he is good. Like other gods, she thinks, the God of Elijah can be easily offended; she has obviously done something to incur his wrath and her son has paid the price.

I have to admit that it takes much less dire circumstances for me to start questioning God's character. I find it all too easy to think that God is more inclined to remind people of their sin, and punish them for it, than he is to demonstrate grace and compassion. And given the success of books like Philip Yancey's *What's So Amazing About Grace?*, I don't think I am alone in that.

One way to change this mindset is to continue to prayerfully read the Bible, where page after page, in stories like this one, God shows that he is, first and foremost, 'compassionate and gracious... slow to anger, abounding in love and faithfulness' (Exodus 34:6). This is nowhere more evident than in the life of Jesus.

Back in our story, notice how Elijah does not try to answer the woman's accusations. Instead, he takes the boy to his room ('the upper room') and prays. In response, God raises the boy from the dead – showing not only his extraordinary power, but also his abundant tender grace for this bereaved widow.

As you read and pray with this issue of *The Upper Room*, may you, like the widow at Zarephath, also come to know the Lord as he truly is.

Daniele Och
UK editor

Solid as a rock

Read 1 Peter 2:4–10

'I tell you that you are Peter, and on this rock I will build my church, and the gates of Hades will not overcome it.'
Matthew 16:18 (NIV)

As a child, I developed a fascination with rocks. I would wander the desert areas around my home picking up rocks of all shapes and sizes. My rock collections would line the window sills at home or pile up on the back porch. I could hold a rock in my hand and imagine that it may have been formed in the fire of a mighty volcano or through the pressure of an ancient sea. I also tried to imagine how God put all these things in motion, resulting in the rock I held in my hand.

In the quoted verse from Matthew, Jesus recognised the inner strength of his disciple and calls him Peter, which translates to 'rock' in Greek. Even solid rock has its cracks, flaws and imperfections. But despite his imperfections, Peter went on to spread the good news wherever he went.

What about me? I tend to have far more flaws and imperfections than I would like to admit. Still, I ask myself, *Am I strong enough, like a solid rock, to be the foundation of love and forgiveness that Jesus has called me to be?* Thankfully, through the grace of God, I don't have to be perfect to fulfil God's purposes for my life.

Prayer: *God of grace, guide us on a path that leads us to an unshakable faith, as solid as a rock. In the name of Jesus, the living cornerstone. Amen*

Thought for the day: I don't have to be perfect to fulfil God's purpose for my life.

Doug Wingert (Arizona, USA)

PRAYER FOCUS: THOSE WORRIED ABOUT THEIR IMPERFECTIONS

Remaining hopeful

Read Mark 5:21–34

He said to her, 'Daughter, your faith has made you well; go in peace, and be healed of your disease.'

Mark 5:34 (NRSV)

Several years ago, my wife and I were trying to have a second child. When she experienced three miscarriages in three years, we did not understand. We were disappointed and confused. But even though our hearts were sad, we found strength and continued to hope in the unlimited power of the Lord Jesus.

Every morning, we prayed and had quiet time to renew our strength. We were particularly encouraged by the story of the woman in today's scripture reading. She remained hopeful that she would be made well, even after twelve years. Her story and her faith encouraged my wife and me to continue believing that God would answer our prayers.

One day, our church held a revival meeting. During an altar call, people who had experienced miscarriage were prayed for. A few months later, my wife became pregnant again. Although she experienced bleeding and needed to go on bed rest during her pregnancy, our second child was born healthy. Like the woman who was healed after twelve years, we continued to hope in the Lord, and what we experienced was a blessing.

Prayer: *Faithful God, we praise you. Thank you for teaching us always to hope and believe in you. In the name of the Lord Jesus, we pray. Amen*

Thought for the day: Even when I don't understand, I will continue to trust and hope in God.

Wardes (Jakarta, Indonesia)

Bookends

Read Ecclesiastes 4:9–12

Carry each other's burdens and so you will fulfil the law of Christ.
Galatians 6:2 (CEB)

I love listening to our church choir as their voices lead us in praise from the chancel. For me, they are also a visible reminder of what praying as a community can do.

Years ago, my husband sang in the choir. He stood beside an older gentleman who was unsteady on his feet and whose legs sometimes gave out. On the other side of this man stood another young man, a good friend of ours. As the choir stood to sing, my husband and our friend were like bookends for the man between them, ready to catch him if his legs gave way. Every time we rose to sing, I watched the three men orchestrate their rise and descent.

To this day, I see the image of them in my mind as I offer prayers for my family, friends, neighbours and country. I thank God for the people who buttress me with their prayers, helping and sustaining me when I falter. This is a great comfort we are able to offer each other.

Prayer: *Loving God, thank you for our companions. Make us aware of those around us who need to be supported by both prayer and acts of compassion. Amen*

Thought for the day: My prayers can help steady the faith of others.

Andrea Doering (New York, USA)

New thatch

Read Psalm 51:1–12

'He who began a good work in you will carry it on to completion until the day of Christ Jesus.'
Philippians 1:6 (NIV)

An old cottage in our village needed new thatch, as the original was in bad shape. Removing the old thatch was a messy, time-consuming business, but it needed to be done properly before the new could be added.

I thought work would start on the ridge and gradually move down, but in fact it was the opposite. This took a long time and at first it seemed that the master thatchers were not doing a very tidy job. I had reservations about what the finished job would look like. But I needn't have worried, as only when all the straw was in place was it trimmed and started to look like I had initially expected. The finished roof is a sight to behold, a perfect finish.

Maturing as a Christian is painful and costly. Our old way of life is removed as we repent of our sins and ask the Lord to cleanse our hearts. Our lifestyle, behaviour and mindset need to change, but usually this does not happen overnight and our lives may look messy at times. We are a work in progress. Yet the grace of God works in our hearts and we become changed, a work of art.

Re-thatching the cottage took around three weeks. The work in us will take a lifetime, but in the hands of the Master Craftsman it will be worth it.

Prayer: *Dear Lord, please make me the best that I can be, more like Jesus my Saviour and friend. Amen*

Thought for the day: How does the Lord want me to change?

Ann Armstrong (England, United Kingdom)

God's helping ways

Read Isaiah 55:8–11

Trust in the Lord with all your heart and lean not on your own understanding.
Proverbs 3:5 (NIV)

One day a woman in our senior living community hurried down to my office. As the assistant manager, I listened as she told me about the sudden spray of water coming from under her bathroom sink. Then I ran up to the second floor with the woman following, but instead of going into her apartment, I entered the one next door. The woman protested that I was entering the wrong apartment. I said, 'I know,' and proceeded to enter her neighbour's apartment anyway. I knew nothing about plumbing, but what I did know made all the difference.

Earlier that morning I had phoned for a plumber, and I knew he was working on a problem in the neighbouring apartment. I suspected the two problems were related, but more importantly, I knew I could immediately produce a plumber to deal with the woman's situation.

I could easily empathise with the woman's confusion. So often I do not see the whole picture. When we give our problems over to God, we may wonder, *How will God help? Why is this happening instead of that?* We often have our own ideas about how to solve a problem, but God sees the big picture. We can trust God to guide us through.

Prayer: *Thank you, God, for all the ways you help us. Your ways are better than ours. Help us trust in you today. Amen*

Thought for the day: God's way is the best way.

Kim Louise Clarke (Alberta, Canada)

Quiet moments

Read Psalm 148:1–14

Sun and moon, praise God! All of you bright stars, praise God!
Psalm 148:3 (CEB)

Sunrise walks are an important spiritual and physical exercise for me. Sometimes I wake before dawn with the sense that the Creator has something to show me. And I'm never disappointed as I step out under fathomless stars and into the calm, pre-dawn air.

Often I give voice to the spontaneous and heartfelt prayer of thanksgiving that rises within me. I understand how the beauty and magnitude of God's creation could elicit the psalmist's cry: 'Sun and moon, praise God! All of you bright stars, praise God!' When a guiding star or clear crescent moon adorns the night sky, I'm especially glad to have been invited to witness God's handiwork.

In the stillness of these early morning moments, I sense God's presence. I become aware of the calm that surrounds me in this place on this planet at this hour, and I'm grateful to God for leading me to this moment. With my soul stilled, I give praise and ask for guidance in my Christian walk.

Prayer: *Thank you, God, for quiet moments in the beauty of your creation. Open our hearts to your promptings be still before you. Amen*

Thought for the day: When my soul is still, I become receptive to God's presence.

Joann Wilson (Nebraska, USA)

My shadow

Read Matthew 28:16–20

'I am with you always, to the very end of the age.'
Matthew 28:20 (NIV)

Running has always been part of my life. Even now that I am a senior citizen, God still blesses me with the ability to run three to four times a week and occasionally participate in a race. On sunny days I notice my shadow running with me, coaching me on my stride, posture and pace. However, on cloudy days my shadow is nowhere to be seen. I am left to run on my own.

We can think about God's presence or absence in our lives in a similar way. When life is great, we are happy, the world is wonderful and we feel that God has blessed us. When health problems, marriage troubles, job loss or financial hardships arise, we may ask, 'Where are you God? Why aren't you here with me?'

But even when we cannot perceive it, God is with us 365 days a year, caring for us and watching over us, no matter what we are experiencing. And God will be there with us until the end of our life's race.

Prayer: *Dear Lord, help us to remember that you are always with us and that you will see us through each day. We pray as Jesus taught us, 'Our Father in heaven, hallowed be your name, your kingdom come, your will be done, on earth as it is in heaven. Give us today our daily bread. And forgive us our debts, as we also have forgiven our debtors. And lead us not into temptation, but deliver us from the evil one' (Matthew 6:9–13). Amen*

Thought for the day: God is with me always.

Ron Lutz (Ohio, USA)

Turning to scripture

Read Psalm 18:30–36

Faith cometh by hearing, and hearing by the word of God.
Romans 10:17 (KJV)

Watching TV and spending time on social media were starting to have a negative effect on me. Everywhere I looked, I seemed to find bad news – people infected by a disease, a recent earthquake, a shooting, people who had recently lost their lives. With each passing day, fear and worry began to creep into my mind. Eventually, I found it hard to leave my house. My emotions were fluctuating, but I seemed to be heading more towards sadness.

My 'faith tank' was getting low, and I asked myself, *What should I be giving my attention to instead?* The one thing that helped me was listening to God's word. Day by day, I began spending more time studying scripture; I listened to sermons and teachings; I sang and danced along to worship music. Although I did not experience an instant change, I kept at it. The more I listened to God's word, the better I felt and the more confident I became. With time, the fear and heaviness left. Spending time in God's word can help move us beyond our fears and is always worthwhile.

Prayer: *Merciful God, we thank you for your word, which builds us up and dispels our fear. Thank you for the loving protection you provide. Amen*

Thought for the day: When I feel worn down and afraid, I will turn to scripture.

Selina Machado (Blantyre, Malawi)

A spiritual forest

Read Galatians 5:16–26

Blessed are those who trust in the Lord, whose trust is the Lord. They shall be like a tree planted by water, sending out its roots by the stream. It shall not fear when heat comes, and its leaves shall stay green; in the year of drought it is not anxious, and it does not cease to bear fruit.

Jeremiah 17:7–8 (NRSV)

I am from a region known for abundant pine forests that stretch for miles. But the forests did not grow overnight. The daily growth of a tree seems indiscernable, but day by day it grows nonetheless. Tiny seeds slowly become saplings; saplings become mature trees. Roots, trunks, branches and verdant needles grow until they form a forest.

Like a forest, spiritual growth happens over time. Such growth requires regular, thoughtful focus on God's word. Our spiritual journey needs constant effort. The world is full of distractions which can cause great anxiety. Emails demand immediate attention. Social media feeds create feelings of inadequacy, dissatisfaction and isolation. The news cycle never ends its bombardment of stories of violence, hate and political and economic woes.

Daily habits of spiritual growth allow us to turn off the noise of life. Just as the slow and steady growth of trees can produce an entire forest, steady growth in our spiritual lives cultivates a healthy connection with God. Pausing daily to reflect, meditate and pray leaves us less anxious and more able to bear the fruit of God's Spirit.

Prayer: *Dear Lord, help us to quiet the distractions of life so that we can grow closer to you. In the name of Jesus. Amen*

Thought for the day: Daily meditation and prayer allow me to bear the fruit of the Spirit (see Galatians 5:22–23).

Keith Ball (Mississippi, USA)

Looking ahead

Read Philippians 3:12–21

Let us run with perseverance the race that is set before us, looking to Jesus, the pioneer and perfecter of faith.
Hebrews 12:1–2 (NRSV)

A sign in front of a church caught my eye one day. It said, 'Don't stumble on something behind you.'

Stumble on something behind me? We usually stumble on things in front of us. But the sign reminded me that we can get derailed by focusing too much on the past, which prevents us from living our lives fully as God intends.

In his letter to the Philippians, Paul wrote that our faith journey is like running a race. Finishing requires that we not look back with regret on what we did that we are ashamed of or what we didn't do that we should have.

Had Paul been fixated on his past – a past in which he persecuted Christians – it is unlikely that he could have spread the good news of Christ to so many new churches. Paul had to press forward with his new life, a life made all the more meaningful because of his commitment to the Lord. We too can avoid stumbling on our past if we keep our eyes on Jesus, the true 'pioneer and perfecter' of our faith.

Prayer: *Dear God, help us remember that our real purpose and meaning comes from you. In Jesus' name we pray. Amen*

Thought for the day: Focusing on Christ helps me to keep moving forward.

Phillip Clark (Rhode Island, USA)

A special prize

Read Isaiah 40:6–11

The grass withers and the flowers fall, but the word of our God endures forever.
Isaiah 40:8 (NIV)

'Well done! You can choose a prize,' I told my student after he won our spelling game. I had collected a variety of treats to offer as prizes for our educational games. Among the prizes were pencils, notebooks and second-hand books that the school didn't need anymore. I couldn't bear to throw away the outdated books or send them to a charity shop when I knew our own students desperately needed educational resources themselves.

Excitedly, my young student rummaged around the bag. He picked out an illustrated children's Bible, and his eyes lit up. He carried it with him, showing it to everyone. He seemed fascinated by the illustrations and stories. During break time, he asked if he could take the Bible outside with him and read it in the gazebo. He normally spent his break racing around the playground, but he spent this one absorbed in his reading.

This second-hand children's Bible might have been forgotten on a shelf. Instead, it became a young boy's precious prize and a witness to others.

Prayer: *Loving Father, thank you for giving us your holy word. Teach us to appreciate it. Amen*

Thought for the day: I will take time to appreciate God's word today.

Cindy Lee (England, United Kingdom)

A change of plan

Read Jeremiah 29:10–14

'I know the plans I have for you,' declares the Lord, 'plans to prosper you and not to harm you, plans to give you hope and a future.'
Jeremiah 29:11 (NIV)

As a student in my early 20s, I knew the plans I had for my life. However, not one of those plans happened. I can see now that over a number of years, God patiently detached me from the paths I thought my life would take. Despite the pain and confusion then, God's leading drew me into over 30 years of Christian ministry in the Anglican Church, something that I could never have imagined happening. It has been at times very challenging and exhausting, but also an enormous privilege and blessing.

And then, over 40 years on, while I was active in ministry and absorbed in a busy and fulfilling life with good, supportive friendships, God threw me another curve ball. A radio interview produced an instant connection with the host that led to marriage and a further total change to life. There have been challenges here, too, but also great blessing and joy as we share life and faith together.

The verse from Jeremiah 29 asserts that God's plans are 'to prosper you and not to harm you, to give you hope and a future'. In a world in chaos, or in the midst of personal crisis or struggle, it can be hard to hold on to that promise. But God's will is always for our good and by looking back we can recognise how he has been faithful and has blessed us with his plans.

Prayer: *Father God, whatever our situation, may we find faith today to trust you and your plans for us to give us hope and a future.*

Thought for the day: The God of surprises has more for me than I can imagine.

Mercia Flanagan (Northern Ireland, United Kingdom)

Closer to God

Read Psalm 86:1–7

I sought the Lord and he answered me. He delivered me from all my fears.
Psalm 34:4 (CEB)

While working diligently to pursue financial security, I grew apart from God. Then I was devastated when I received my diagnosis: lupus, a disease that attacks the body's immune system. In my case, it seriously affected my lungs. Due to the multiple recurring complications involved, I went to the clinic many times. With each visit, I lived with the uncertainty of my survival.

With the complexities unique to this condition and the ensuing depression, I cried out to the Lord to help me. I wanted to believe once more in God's promises. My health began to improve. Even more extraordinary was the fact that this situation allowed me to draw closer to God again and to share with others the wonder of God's power to change all things. Thanks be to God!

Prayer: *Merciful God, in our distress you hear our cries. Thank you for your love and grace that creates change in our hearts and allows us to trust in your promises for our good. Amen*

Thought for the day: God always listens to my prayers.

Yolika del Carmen Maurera Sosa (Texas, USA)

Unforgettable generosity

Read Acts 9:36–43

Remember this: whoever sows sparingly will also reap sparingly, and whoever sows generously will also reap generously.

2 Corinthians 9:6 (NIV)

My mother had a heart of empathy, generosity and compassion. After she got married, she became a caregiver for her husband and his family. When she cooked, she always prepared extra food in case relatives stopped by. She cared for other families in our neighbourhood. And she often visited people who were sick or lonely and took them food. After my father's death, she lived with and cared for my family. My children have fond memories of her kind, gentle heart and the delicious curries she would prepare. I feel blessed that she was my mother.

When I think of my mother's legacy, I am reminded of Tabitha from Acts 9. She was known for her good works and for helping others. Following Tabitha's death, Peter found many widows grieving. When Peter prayed and told her to get up, Tabitha opened her eyes and got up. Word of this miracle spread and caused many to believe.

Generosity is a gift from God. Our world is fraught with injustice and an imbalance of resources. But as instruments of God's grace, we can bring comfort to others by practising generosity wherever we go.

Prayer: *Dear Lord, help us to love you and follow your example of humility and generosity. Give us wisdom and courage to respond to the needs of others. In Christ's holy name. Amen*

Thought for the day: Today I will practise generosity as a follower of Christ.

Navamani Peter (Karnataka, India)

In the potter's hand

Read Jeremiah 18:1–6

*House of Israel, can't I deal with you like this potter, declares the Lord?
Like clay in the potter's hand, so are you in mine.*
Jeremiah 18:6 (CEB)

Ten years ago, I made a decision that had a devastating effect on my family – the loss of my marriage, the loss of my career and a four-year stint in the criminal justice system, including two years of incarceration. Although my prison time is over, my status as a convicted felon will never end. My family also carries that stigma. They will forever have the scars left by this ordeal.

As I contemplate the last decade and all my family and I have been through, I am drawn to the passage in Jeremiah where God sent the prophet to the potter's house to receive a divine message. The potter was working on a pot that was imperfect, so he formed it into another pot. The message was clear: God can take our imperfect selves and shape us into something new.

Ten years ago, I could be identified as a father, husband, business owner, CPA and provider. Today, I am identified as a servant, employee, writer, friend and comforter. I have realised we must be willing and receptive if God is going to shape us into something new. God's work takes time, and we must be patient while we persevere in trusting our Creator.

Prayer: *Dear God, strengthen us to surrender to your potter's hand, to be moulded into the people you desire us to be. Amen*

Thought for the day: Today I will begin to let God mould me into a new creation.

Steve Wakefield (Alabama, USA)

Always on God's mind

Read 1 Kings 19:3–13

Many, Lord my God, are the wonders you have done, the things you planned for us.
Psalm 40:5 (NIV)

While visiting my husband's family in the suburbs of Melbourne, Australia, we were sitting in the backyard before dinner. Four-year-old Jesse skipped around the edges of our conversation, seemingly lost in his own little world. He squirmed as we ate our meal and then slipped out of the room. Suddenly Jesse reappeared and thrust a purple piece of construction paper at me with a rush of words. I was puzzled, so he spoke in a louder voice, 'It's a bird, and I love you.' Yes, two large eyes were recognisable and a very large beak.

That moment with a young boy reminded me of how often we nearly miss God's voice saying much the same thing. 'It's sunrise over a new day, and I love you.' Or 'It's a terrible loss, but I am here and I love you.' It is the same quiet voice of the one who spoke to the despondent prophet Elijah in today's scripture reading.

Our attention may be elsewhere when God hands us a love note. Worried or distracted, we may glance at the words without comprehension. Yet God persists. As the quoted scripture reminds us, we are always on God's mind.

I framed Jesse's picture and hung it by my desk. Its huge eyes and funny beak are a reminder to me that God's eyes are on us. Firmly in God's gaze, our hearts are comforted and reassured.

Prayer: *Dear Lord, help us not to be distracted from your voice but always to be attentive to your Spirit. Amen*

Thought for the day: Today I will listen for the quiet voice of God.

Debra Celovsky (California, USA)

Everything we need

Read Exodus 4:1–17

The Lord said to him, 'What's that in your hand?' Moses replied, 'A shepherd's rod.'
Exodus 4:2 (CEB)

Moses felt unequipped for the task God placed in front of him. However, in God's eyes, Moses had what he needed – a rod. With that rod, Moses performed miracles in Egypt and used it to part the Red Sea, allowing the Israelites to pass through. That same rod brought Joshua victory in battle. And it made water gush from a rock. What Moses overlooked, God used to shape the course of history.

Today, God is asking the same question of us that God asked Moses: 'What is in your hand?' It could be a pen, cooking utensil, computer, ball, phone, certificate, diploma or small plot of land. We should not dismiss what we have, no matter how small or unworthy it may seem. God is ready to use it to fulfil God's purpose in our lives.

God created us that we may serve. We read in scripture that there is much harvest on God's farm, but harvesters are few. And God is calling on us. Let us embrace the tools God has given us so that we may be ready and willing to serve. God will transform that which we see as 'just a rod' into something great for God's glory.

Prayer: *God of possibilities, thank you for the gifts you have given us. Teach us to see the value in what we have and to use it to serve you. Amen*

Thought for the day: God can use the gifts I undervalue to serve others.

Mary Charles (Nairobi City, Kenya)

'Daddy fix!'

Read Psalm 34:17–19

God so loved the world that he gave his only Son, so that everyone who believes in him won't perish but will have eternal life.
John 3:16 (CEB)

When I was a small child and one of my toys broke, I would carry it to my dad, hold it up and confidently say, 'Daddy fix!' Over the years, I became the daddy who fixed things when my own children broke them. Even though I am now older and my dad has gone on to heaven, I have come to realise that I still have a Father I can trust to fix the broken things in my life – even me.

The Bible is replete with times when our heavenly Father helped his children, as well as with promises that our Father will continue to do so. Think of God leading his children out of slavery in Egypt to the freedom of the promised land; of Jesus as he healed the sick, gave sight to the blind and raised the dead. To me, the most profound of these examples is John 3:16, where it says God gave us Jesus, our way to eternal life.

Surely God will not instantly fix every broken thing in our lives. But God will walk with us, comfort us and sometimes carry us through our troubles and sufferings – fixing them in God's way and time.

Prayer: *Heavenly Father, help us always remember that you are here to help us – all we need to do is ask. Be with us as we walk our path today. When we stumble, comfort us, guide us and help us to know you love us always. Amen*

Thought for the day: Whatever is broken in our lives, God's love can mend.

Kim Koratsky (Tennessee, USA)

A strong foundation

Read Luke 6:46–49

No one can lay any foundation other than the one already laid, which is Jesus Christ.
1 Corinthians 3:11 (NIV)

When my husband began building our house, I was eager to help. He gave me the job of mixing the mortar for the basement block he was laying. Mortar is a paste which hardens to fill the gaps between blocks and to bind them together. My husband, who has made mortar many times, told me to combine three shovelfuls of sand, one shovelful of mortar mix, a little bit of cement and about half a pail of water. After hearing the mixing instructions, I had questions: *How big is a shovelful? How much is a little bit?* I had not practised making the mortar, and I was worried that it wouldn't be strong enough to hold together the foundation of our home.

Our lives also need a strong foundation, and Jesus is that foundation. In today's scripture reading, Jesus instructs his followers not only to hear his words but to act on them. Through practice, he says, his followers would be like a wise man that built his foundation on a rock. Without practice, our faith can be shaken when trouble comes. Prayer, Bible study, serving God and being part of a Christian community are all practices that can help us to build, repair and maintain a strong spiritual foundation. With a strong spiritual foundation, we will be able to stand firm during the tests and trials of life.

Prayer: *Dear God, thank you for Jesus, our rock and our strong foundation. In his name, we pray. Amen*

Thought for the day: Jesus is my rock and my foundation.

Mary B. Erva (Michigan, USA)

Live confidently

Read John 6:54–69

In peace I will lie down and sleep, for you alone, Lord, make me dwell in safety.
Psalm 4:8 (NIV)

Every evening before I go to sleep, my thoughts turn to the Lord as I meditate on Psalm 4:8. In this frame of mind, I go to sleep with ease. Some of my peace of mind comes from safety I have created for myself: a secure house, insurance and savings for unexpected expenses. But to truly live with confidence, I need something I can't procure on my own. Confidence can't be purchased. It is a gift from God.

That is why I can sleep in peace, knowing that God will give us the gift of tomorrow and tomorrow will take care of itself. God promises that even when problems seem insurmountable, nothing is impossible for God. Emotionally and spiritually, I can find rest because I trust in the Lord's promise. This peace is a gift from God – a gift that allows us to move forward each day and live confidently.

Prayer: *Almighty Lord, you are all-knowing, and your words reassure us. Show us how to live confidently and faithfully according to your teachings. We pray the prayer Jesus taught us, 'Our Father which art in heaven, Hallowed be thy name. Thy kingdom come. Thy will be done, as in heaven, so in earth. Give us day by day our daily bread. And forgive us our sins; for we also forgive every one that is indebted to us. And lead us not into temptation; but deliver us from evil' (Luke 11:2–4, KJV). Amen*

Thought for the day: My trust in God is complete. God will not fail me.

Juan Gattinoni (Buenos Aires, Argentina)

Free in Christ

Read Luke 18:18–19

A person is not justified by the works of the law, but by faith in Jesus Christ. So we, too, have put our faith in Christ Jesus that we may be justified by faith in Christ and not by the works of the law, because by the works of the law no one will be justified.
Galatians 2:16 (NIV)

Growing up in a family of overachievers, I always felt one step behind. I was not an all-A student, and I did not want to make decisions about my future based on how much money I would make. I wanted to take my own path in life, but I was surrounded by people who constantly put me down for my lack of societal perfection. I began to feel worthless, as if my life had no meaning. But I soon realised that I must not wallow in these worldly flaws. I was created in God's perfect image; I could rejoice in my differences. It was vital for me to recognise that through Jesus, I am free from the expectations of society.

Genesis 1:27 states that humans are made in the image of God. Yet, society has created standards for humanity that can lead us to doubt God's beautiful creation. We do not need to justify ourselves by social expectations; we are justified by our faith in Jesus Christ. In Jesus, we are free to be who God created us to be.

Prayer: *Faithful God, thank you for creating me in your image and for freeing me from the expectations of society. Amen*

Thought for the day: I am perfect in the eyes of God.

Lara Jarrous (Texas, USA)

More than we can bear

Read Matthew 11:28–30

'Come to me, all you who are weary and burdened, and I will give you rest.'
Matthew 11:28 (NIV)

For 42 years I had the privilege of serving as a pastor. I officiated at many funerals and ministered to many people going through trying and tragic situations. Often I heard well-meaning people make statements that made me cringe. One such statement was 'God will never give you more than you can handle.'

In my experience, we do go through trials that are more than we can bear. In 1 Corinthians 10:13, Paul wrote, 'God is faithful, and he will not let you be tested beyond your strength.' But we often overlook the second half of that verse: 'but with the testing he will also provide the way out so that you may be able to endure it.' We may experience trials that are too much for us to handle on our own, but with God's help we can endure them.

Jesus says, 'Come to me, all you who are weary and burdened, and I will give you rest… my yoke is easy and my burden is light' (Matthew 11:28–30). Jesus is speaking to those of us who are carrying burdens much too heavy to shoulder alone. And in those few words he reveals that when we experience such burdens we can trust God enough to hand them over to our Creator. Nothing is too heavy for God to carry!

Prayer: *Heavenly Father, help us to release our concerns, burdens and needs into your care. Amen*

Thought for the day: With God's help I can endure my trials.

Thomas Broadhead (Texas, USA)

PRAYER FOCUS: THOSE EXPERIENCING TRAGEDY

Closer to God

Read John 15:1–8

'I will give you a new heart and put a new spirit in you. I will remove your stony heart from your body and replace it with a living one.'
Ezekiel 36:26 (CEB)

One day, my coworker gave me a potted flower that was slightly dry. I knew that if the plant was not watered, it would soon die. So I began to care for the flower by watering it every day and placing it in the sunlight. Soon the flower was refreshed and grew even more beautiful.

This reminds me how much God loves us. Often we may feel neglected, lost or even like there is no hope for us. But when we draw closer to God and let God douse our dry hearts with the Holy Spirit, we are renewed. When we feel that God is far from our lives, the truth is that God has never left us – even when we have left God. God's love is permanent and eternal.

Let us continue to draw our hearts and minds closer to God so that we can become the persons God desires us to be. We know that God, the source of life, will help us with every struggle we face.

Prayer: *Loving God, soften our hearts so that we may become more Christlike. Teach us to live your word so that we may grow to know you more deeply. Amen*

Thought for the day: God is always near, waiting for me to draw closer.

Titik Rahayuningsih (Indonesia)

No prestige needed

Read 1 Samuel 17:41–50

When the Philistine looked David over, he sneered at David because he was just a boy.
1 Samuel 17:42 (CEB)

When I meet new people, they are rarely impressed when I tell them that I work as a cleaning lady in a nursing home. Evidently, making beds and mopping floors doesn't sound like an exciting mission field for Christ. Nevertheless, manual labour is what God has called me to do. Over the years I have come to understand three important things: my workplace is filled with lonely people, lonely people love talking to the janitor, and proclaiming the power of Christ does not require an elevated platform.

In 1 Samuel, we learn that David was a shepherd. Because David's job wasn't prestigious and he was young and inexperienced, Goliath had nothing but disdain for him. However, once on the battlefield, the young man who loved his lambs was able to knock out the giant with a single, well-aimed stone. David's story teaches us that no matter who we are or what we do, we should not disregard the importance of God's calling for us.

Prayer: *Dear heavenly Father, thank you for calling us to serve you. When we feel timid, help us feel your hand guiding us, empowering us to battle giants and succeed in your purposes. Fill us with your Spirit, and enable us to bring glory to you. Amen*

Thought for the day: Only God can measure my worth.

Geo PicKell (North Dakota, USA)

Moving on

Read Isaiah 43:18–21

'Forget the former things; do not dwell on the past. See, I am doing a new thing!'
Isaiah 43:18–19 (NIV)

I identify with the baby bird that lingers in its nest outside my door. Its three siblings flew away yesterday, and it is alone. Its parents flutter by in the mornings and evenings, sometimes providing food, but mostly urging the little one to spread its wings and fly. But the baby bird is hesitant. Over and over it hops to the edge of the nest, looks around and down, and then retreats to the only place it has known.

I identify with that baby bird because I have been afraid to move on so many times. Whether it is beginning school for the first time, changing schools, leaving home, getting married, beginning a new job, moving to a new place or retiring, life is filled with uncertainty. It is easy to hop to the edge of my comfortable nest, look around and want to retreat to the security of what I know.

But just as God promised the people in today's scripture reading, God will always be doing new things, always providing a way, always giving us fresh reasons to move out to do God's bidding and to proclaim God's love. Because God is our shelter, we can step to the edge of our nests, open our wings and fly with confidence in a faithful God.

Prayer: *O God, give me courage today to move out of my place of comfort and move on to the opportunities and relationships you have prepared for me. Amen*

Thought for the day: I can move on to new things because God moves with me.

Jerry White (Florida, USA)

God's love

Read Romans 8:31–39

Who will separate us from the love of Christ? Will affliction or distress or persecution or famine or nakedness or peril or sword?
Romans 8:35 (NRSV)

I vividly remember the day I received bad news from back home. I was in seminary in a foreign country, and at that moment I felt lost and in despair. I could not help but ask, *Where is God when it hurts? Where was God when all these things were taking place in my life?* I believe that life brings hard circumstances to us all. But God cares deeply about each of us. God spoke and is still speaking to me in the midst of my pain.

In the vast African forest where the seminary is located, I was listening to the songs of the birds and the noise of the bugs when my attention was drawn to Romans 8. I heard God speaking to me through the holy scriptures in the midst of my pain. The first thing we learn from this passage in Romans is that we all go through suffering. That's why the apostle Paul asks, 'Who will separate us?' The answer resounds: no one and nothing can separate us from the love of God! God's love outweighs the pain. Sometimes God delivers us from the pain and other times God delivers us in the pain. No matter what the circumstances, we find ourselves surrounded by God's love.

Prayer: *Caring God, surround us always with your love. Amen*

Thought for the day: Nothing can separate me from God's love.

Felisberto Dambi (Southern Province, Zambia)

Unity in Christ

Read Ephesians 4:1–16

How good and pleasant it is when God's people live together in unity!
Psalm 133:1 (NIV)

In high school, I didn't fully grasp how important it is to be a part of a Christ-centred community. I heard other students in my church's youth ministry talk about the ways they were growing in their different Christian groups, but I just didn't get it. My focus began to shift from finding people who would encourage my spiritual growth to simply finding more people to hang out with.

When the many superficial relationships I had developed fell apart after graduation, I realised my mistake. I had been searching for the wrong thing. College was the perfect opportunity to try again. Because God had drawn my attention to the superficiality of my high school relationships, I was more aware and better equipped to make deeper connections in college. I was truly ready to work on building a Christ-centred circle of friends. God directed me to my current group of friends, and I have been able to grow in my faith in tremendous ways. Now I understand the power of having people to keep you accountable, to encourage you and to remind you of God's love.

Prayer: *Dear God, thank you for giving us the opportunity to share your love with others and the opportunity to receive that love. Help us to find others who can encourage growth in our relationship with you. Amen*

Thought for the day: God calls me to find a Christ-centred community.

Kaiya Matthews (Texas, USA)

Divine helper

Read John 14:15–27

'I will ask the Father, and he will give you another advocate to help you and be with you forever.'
John 14:16 (NIV)

My grandfather had always been a source of inspiration to me. Though he was not very literate, he was a godly man. At a young age, he was invited to speak to a congregation. The invitation was a great honour, but it also brought him anxiety. The idea of addressing a large group of scholarly people made him nervous. As the day approached, he prayed, asking God to give him the courage to deliver the speech. When the day came, he stood up to speak. When he received a round of applause, he realised that he had delivered a good message. Later he told me that he felt like the Holy Spirit was speaking through him and that the words came out of him like a flowing stream.

Before his ascension, Jesus promised to send an advocate. The disciples were at times hopeless and helpless, but the Holy Spirit showed up and changed everything. The group gathered at Pentecost that day in the upper room was renewed with great courage and began speaking in a variety of languages. The Holy Spirit helped the disciples in their distress, and the same Holy Spirit is within us. In moments of doubt, weakness or fear, we can ask God for help. When we have no words to pray, we can simply ask God to send the Holy Spirit to deliver and comfort us.

Prayer: *Dear Lord, fill us with your Holy Spirit so that we may receive your divine help in every adversity. Amen*

Thought for the day: I believe in the power of the Holy Spirit.

Hitesh J. Solanki (Gujarat, India)

Turbulence ahead

Read Matthew 8:23–27

The men were amazed and asked, 'What kind of man is this? Even the winds and the waves obey him!'
Matthew 8:27 (NIV)

As we began our cross-country trip, the pilot came on the intercom and announced, 'We are expecting some turbulence at the start of our trip, so we would like you to keep your seat belts fastened. It should last only about ten minutes.' He then continued, 'We may get some more turbulence about halfway into our flight, and we are expecting thunderstorms in the afternoon near our destination.' The seat belt sign came on shortly after takeoff and remained on.

I imagined all kinds of terrible situations, including the plane's breaking apart in severe turbulence! For worriers like me this is often the case – our imagination takes over. But at some point in the journey, I recalled the story of Jesus and the disciples in the boat in the midst of a storm. Jesus calmed the wind and the waves – and the hearts of the disciples. I imagined Jesus sitting next to me on the plane, saying, 'It will be okay. I am here with you.' Then I relaxed.

The turbulence was only mild, but what I imagined might happen was much worse. We who sometimes picture disaster can also picture the comforting, calming presence of the Lord. Storms will come, but imagining Jesus with us in those storms can calm our hearts and prepare us for whatever lies ahead.

Prayer: *God who calmed the sea, you promise to be with us, even in rough seas and turbulent times. Be with us now and give us peace, no matter what lies ahead. In Jesus' name. Amen*

Thought for the day: In every storm, Jesus is my calming presence.

Mike C. Bertoglio (Georgia, USA)

God's comfort

Read 2 Corinthians 1:3–7

[God] comforts us in all our troubles, so that we can comfort those in any trouble with the comfort we ourselves receive from God.
2 Corinthians 1:4 (NIV)

I began having severe panic attacks in my mid-30s. Within weeks I was admitted to a psychiatric hospital and diagnosed with bipolar disorder. I had no history of mental illness, so this experience was frightening. A great doctor, the right medications and a change in diet stabilised my system but didn't answer my deeper questions. Where was God, and what was my role in the healing process?

I became more active in my church. I devoured scripture, and I looked for God everywhere. I kept a gratitude journal and learned to give thanks in all circumstances (1 Thessalonians 5:18). I deepened my prayer life. My faith grew, and I sought to love and forgive others and myself more. Sixteen years later, God delivered me from fear.

God heals us, but not always in our time or on our terms. I still have bipolar disorder, but in Christ, my soul is more at peace than before my breakdown. I no longer have mood swings, and I'm defined more by my courage. My long journey through the wilderness prepared me to answer God's call: 'Comfort, comfort my people, says your God' (Isaiah 40:1). Other people's struggles may differ from mine, but by offering the comfort I've received from God, I can help others find their own way home.

Prayer: *Thank you, Lord, for the many ways you comfort us. By your grace, help us to extend your comfort to others. Amen*

Thought for the day: How will I offer God's comfort to others today?

Barbara Gail Bliss (Colorado, USA)

A grateful heart

Read Philippians 1:3–6

I thank my God every time I remember you.
Philippians 1:3 (NIV)

Reflecting on my spiritual journey, I realise certain people have helped to shape the direction of my life. I remember the pastor who shared the gospel with me when I was a young agnostic. I remember the young adult group at church who welcomed me, and I remember the vice principal of a seminary who stepped in to help a new student whose family was going through a time of fragile finances. Some of those memories go back 50 years! God brings people into our lives who encourage us and guide us in life-changing ways. When I remember these people and the blessing they have been, I feel gratitude for them and to God.

The apostle Paul felt this kind of gratitude. Today's quoted scripture is the beginning of Paul's letter to the church in Philippi. The church supported him in his ministry and sent one of their own with a gift for him when he was under house arrest in Rome. In the book of Philippians, Paul remembers the many blessings he received from the church. Even in prison, he thanks God in his prayers. Like Paul, may we remember how much God has blessed us through others, and may our prayers come from grateful hearts.

Prayer: *Dear God, thank you for the people you have brought into our lives at just the right time. Help us to remember them with a grateful heart. Amen*

Thought for the day: Today I will thank God for the blessings others have brought into my life.

Awlwyn Balnave (British Columbia, Canada)

Finish it later

Read Ephesians 2:4–10

When he had received the sour wine, Jesus said, 'It is completed.'
Bowing his head, he gave up his life.
John 19:30 (CEB)

I often find myself putting off housework and other chores. Even though I am aware of my tendency to procrastinate, I still often find myself with a sink full of dishes left over from the day before. I know that I can do better than this, but I never seem to improve. As a result, I have deep anxiety about how my friends might judge me. *What if they drop in unexpectedly? Worse yet, what if I die suddenly when everything is a mess?*

Sometimes I suffer the same sort of anxiety about my relationship with God. *Will I be prepared when I meet God face to face? What have I left undone? Have I been good enough? How will God judge my time on earth?*

When I experience this kind of spiritual panic, I remind myself that my relationship with God is not like my relationship with housework. Housework is never really finished. In contrast, Jesus left nothing undone when he did his work on the cross. Because I choose to believe in and follow Christ, my sins are erased. There is nothing more I need to do.

Prayer: *Thank you, Lord Jesus, for the salvation you freely give. Help us to trust you, love you and serve you. Reassure us of how secure we are in you. In your name, we pray. Amen*

Thought for the day: I will rest secure in my faith today.

Kathy Reagan Eyler (Tennessee, USA)

Living a parable

Read Luke 15:8–10

'There is rejoicing in the presence of the angels of God over one sinner who repents.'
Luke 15:10 (NIV)

Upon seeing a coin on the ground, I used to pick it up, slip it into my pocket and continue on without another thought. Then I read Luke 15:8–10. In Jesus' parable of the woman and the lost coin, the woman searched diligently throughout her house until she found the coin. She was so happy that she called all her friends and neighbours to come over to rejoice with her. Jesus said the found coin represented a repentant sinner.

I started to think about how I could live out this parable. Each lost coin once belonged to someone, and God knows who they are. I decided that the next time I saw a lost coin, I would pray for the person who lost it, trusting that God knows who they are, where they are and what they need.

Today, as I picked up a lost coin, I prayed something like this, 'Heavenly Father, you know who lost this coin. If that person is lost, then let them be found and brought into your kingdom. And if this one is already part of your family, bless them today that they may rejoice in your goodness. Amen.' Maybe I will get the chance to meet these strangers in heaven, and there we can rejoice together.

Prayer: *O God, show us those who need our help and prayers today. Amen*

Thought for the day: God reminds me to pray for others.

Gary Crabtree (Ohio, USA)

Growing in faith

Read Philippians 4:10–13

I can do all this through him who gives me strength.
Philippians 4:13 (NIV)

I find driving our motor home extremely scary. I worry that I will misjudge the size of the vehicle while driving around roundabouts, along narrow roads and in congested areas. However, I still drive the vehicle, both to share the driving with my husband and so that I know how to drive it in case of an emergency. Each time I do it, I pray, 'Lord, I can't do this. Will you please drive in my place?' After this prayer, I don't drive perfectly or feel totally calm, but I sense the Lord's presence and that God is enabling me to do what I cannot do in my own strength. I still make mistakes while driving, but I learn from them and hopefully become a better driver.

I think this is one of the ways the Lord enables me to grow in faith and trust in him. Jesus compared the kingdom of God to a tiny mustard seed that was planted and grew into a tree so that birds could perch in its branches (see Matthew 13:31–35). Perhaps challenging situations help us grow by strengthening our faith and helping us trust in God. As I grow in faith, I see more of my prayers answered, and so God's kingdom grows.

Prayer: *Dear Lord, help our faith to grow through all the challenges we face today. Thank you for your unfailing presence. Amen*

Thought for the day: Prayer connects me to God's guiding presence.

Gillian Tettmar (England, United Kingdom)

In God's time

Read Isaiah 43:1–7

He has made everything beautiful in its time.
Ecclesiastes 3:11 (NIV)

At the beginning of winter, I took a walk through the woods and was remembering that the trees had been beautiful and full of colourful leaves only a few weeks prior. Now the branches were bare. The field and trees were all the same dull colour. As I took a picture of one tree, I couldn't help but think how dreary it was. Still I noticed little bumps on each branch, and I thought about how those bumps would become tiny buds bringing forth new life in the spring.

I was taking this walk one year after we lost our foster son in a car accident. After the accident, I didn't know how God could possibly redeem the situation. But slowly God reminded me of all the beautiful moments we had shared with our son, and I realised those memories were a gift that could never be taken. We were never promised an indefinite amount of time with our son, but each moment we did have was beautiful. As I've come to terms with the loss, God has used me to help other mothers who have lost their children.

God has a way of working for good even when we can't see it. Sometimes we feel like we are left bare, but God heals our brokenness, allowing new life to spring forth. In God's time, beautiful blessings can grow from our pain and brokenness.

Prayer: *Dear God, thank you for making all things new. You heal our brokenness and make things beautiful again in your time. Amen*

Thought for the day: In time, God will heal my brokenness.

Marci Krull (Iowa, USA)

Looking at the heart

Read 1 Samuel 16:1–7

The Lord said to Samuel, 'Do not consider his appearance or his height, for I have rejected him. The Lord does not look at the things people look at. People look at the outward appearance, but the Lord looks at the heart.'

1 Samuel 16:7 (NIV)

I drove to the school where my wife teaches kindergarten to deliver a package. I opened her classroom door only to find she had stepped out. As I stood in the doorway, one of the students asked, 'Who are you?' My response was, 'Who do you *think* I am?' When a student replied, 'You're her father,' I said, 'No.' Then another student called out, 'You're her grandfather!' Abruptly, I responded, 'I'm her husband!' The students looked bewildered. Apparently, to kindergartners anyone with gray hair is an oldster! Appearances can be misleading.

This was Samuel's experience when the Lord sent him to Bethlehem to anoint the next king of Israel. When Samuel met Jesse's firstborn son, Eliab, Samuel thought, based on Eliab's appearance, *Surely, the Lord's anointed stands before me.* But the Lord rejected Eliab. Then God warned Samuel about judging people by appearance alone: 'The Lord does not look at the things people look at. People look at the outward appearance, but the Lord looks at the heart.'

Appearance alone does not reveal an individual's true self. God values the characteristics of integrity, faith and dependability above a pleasing persona, and we should do the same in assessing the character of others.

Prayer: *O Lord, help us not to judge others by appearance alone but strive to discern their inner qualities. Amen*

Thought for the day: God values my character more than my appearance.

Wayne Greenawalt (Illinois, USA)

Available to all

Read Matthew 19:13–15

'Allow the children to come to me,' Jesus said. 'Don't forbid them, because the kingdom of heaven belongs to people like these children.'
Matthew 19:14 (CEB)

I often think of my younger brother as a child who doesn't really understand. Yet he understands a lot of information better than I do. Young children are often considered unable to understand or do things well. But having this mindset means we can miss the wisdom children have to offer.

In Jesus' day, society looked down upon not only children, but also women, people with disabilities and those who were poor or uneducated. These groups were considered immature in faith or even sinful. So Jesus' words in today's scripture verse challenged the status quo. He welcomed the children, even calling them the heirs of the kingdom of heaven. Jesus was reminding everyone that God's love is not limited to certain groups of people; God accepts *all* people.

As followers of Christ, we are also invited to accept all people. We should not demean the faith of anyone, including young children, for any reason. God's love is available to everyone who seeks God.

Prayer: *Dear God, enable us to love people of all ages and from all walks of life just as you love us. We pray in the name of Christ Jesus. Amen*

Thought for the day: God's love is available to all people.

Ester Novaria (West Java, Indonesia)

Ask the expert

Read Luke 11:5–13
'Everyone who asks receives; the one who seeks finds; and to the one who knocks, the door will be opened.'
Luke 11:10 (NIV)

When I wanted to determine how best to invest my savings, I spoke with a financial advisor. The time I needed to install an outdoor electrical circuit, I hired an electrician. And when my mower broke, I took it to a repair shop. In all of these instances, the task at hand required knowledge and skills beyond my own, so I went to an expert.

So why, then, do I insist on relying on my own knowledge when it comes to other important matters? When I need guidance and understanding about my current situation or the future, no one is more capable than God.

It is good for us to be honest, to ask for God's guidance and to request that God's will for our lives be made clear to us. We can ask and keep asking; seek and keep seeking; knock and keep knocking. Remembering that God often communicates with us through the Bible, may we always go to the best – to God.

Prayer: *Dear God, give us the faith to ask you for wisdom. Open our hearts to receive and follow your guidance. Amen*

Thought for the day: At all times, God is ready to listen to my requests.

Bob LaForge (New Jersey, USA)

Learning curve

Read John 13:12–17

[Nicodemus] came to Jesus at night and said, 'Rabbi, we know you are a teacher who has come from God.'
John 3:2 (NIV)

I recently went through a decluttering exercise, trying to clear out all the articles and papers I promised myself to read at some point, when I came across my old school reports. I dreaded reading them at the time and although many decades had passed, I still felt an unease as I read the comments. 'Lacks attention,' 'Needs to try harder,' 'Must do better' and many other admonishments jumped from the pages. I fed the reports into the shredder!

I then thought of the teachers who wrote those reports. Some of them were good, others not so. However, their aim was to instil in me discipline and knowledge, even though I found it hard to hear at the time.

For both the disciples then and for we his disciples now, Jesus is our teacher, as Jesus himself acknowledges. Open the gospels and his teaching pours from the pages with much for us to learn, digest and act upon. While at times it can be difficult to accept Jesus' message, his is no ordinary teaching. If we have open hearts, we can echo Nicodemus' words: 'We know you are a teacher who has come from God.' There is no greater teacher then Jesus.

Prayer: *Thank you, Lord, for your wisdom and words, which echo through our thoughts and minds. May we cling to your teaching each and every day. Amen*

Thought for the day: May Jesus' teaching instil in me a sense of everlasting excitement.

John Hauselman (England, United Kingdom)

Show kindness

Read Genesis 24:12–27

After she had given him a drink, she said, 'I'll draw water for your camels too, until they have had enough to drink.'
Genesis 24:19 (NIV)

In today's scripture, we read about Rebekah's generosity and kindness to Abraham's servant who was a stranger to her. Her kindness eventually led to her marrying Isaac.

When I was younger, I also experienced the kindness of a stranger. My family and I lived in South Africa. As a Kenyan, I knew well that I was a foreigner, and I was prepared to handle discrimination. One morning, we went to a distant mall with my dad to buy some equipment. When we got to the store, my dad was redirected to a nearby shop. We sat under a tree near the exit of the shopping centre and waited for my dad. While we waited, a white man walked by multiple times and looked at us. We initially assumed he was lost, but after a while we became concerned, and my mother began praying. The man eventually approached us with a smile, had a short talk with my mother, and offered to buy us lunch.

I was amazed by the man's kindness. That day, I decided to show kindness to strangers just as he showed kindness to me and my family. Let us all show kindness to a stranger today. We never know whose life we might change.

Prayer: *Dear God, enable us to be kind to strangers so that they may experience your love through us and know that they are valued. Amen*

Thought for the day: Following Rebekah's example, I will be kind to a stranger today.

Faith Okello (Kajiado County, Kenya)

Not insignificant

Read Matthew 13:31–35

'The kingdom of heaven is like a mustard seed.'
Matthew 13:31 (NIV)

Wanting to get a birthday present for my mother, I walked a mile to the nearest shopping centre and stopped at a department-store jewellery counter. Everything under the glass was either unappealing or more than I could afford with the earnings from my paper route. I found more affordable options on a revolving rack of charms on top of the glass case. A gold charm wrapped around a tiny glass bubble caught my eye. Sealed inside the bubble was a round, brownish speck. The label indicated it was a mustard seed. I remembered that Jesus had compared the kingdom of heaven to a mustard seed, so I bought the charm.

Years later, I re-read Jesus' parable of the mustard seed and remembered that glass-encased seed. If the seed had been released and planted, it could have sprouted and become a flourishing plant.

Jesus compared his kingdom to a mustard seed. Because I am a part of God's kingdom, I am like a mustard seed too. I may be small, but I'm not insignificant. I have received life from Jesus Christ – and more. I have the potential to sprout and grow, as any seed would. And as I grow, by the grace of God, I can provide hope and shelter for those around me.

Prayer: *Liberating Christ, free us from the things which keep us from sprouting and growing so we can provide hope for others. Amen*

Thought for the day: I may be small, but I'm not insignificant.

David R. Schultz (Illinois, USA)

Surrounded by love

Read Psalm 32:8–11

The Lord's unfailing love surrounds the one who trusts in him.
Psalm 32:10 (NIV)

Every morning, I pull on my fluffy, blue robe to keep me warm as I make coffee and settle in for my morning prayers and Bible reading. After finishing my morning routine, I used to hang up my robe with a sigh, already looking forward to wearing it the next day.

Then one morning, I read Psalm 32:10. The word *surround* jumped out at me. I closed my eyes and imagined God's love surrounding me. I pictured a soft, warm light covering me from head to toe. I experienced a deep sense of peace and contentment. And when I hung up my robe that morning, I didn't feel the familiar sadness at leaving my source of comfort behind. I had God's unfailing love surrounding me – a comforting presence that would never leave me.

Now every morning as I put on my robe, its temporary comfort reminds me of God's eternal love. And when I put my robe away, I remember that I'll carry God's love with me all day. When I feel anxious or sad, I visualise God's love covering me and I relax into God's comforting holy presence. What a blessing to know that God's love surrounds us always!

Prayer: *Comforting God, thank you for your eternal, unchanging love that is with us always. Remind us to turn to you for the comfort and peace we crave. Amen*

Thought for the day: God's love and comfort surround me always.

Alyson Rockhold (Texas, USA)

When failure is victory

Read Judges 20:18–28

They asked, 'Shall we go up again to fight against the Benjamites, our fellow Israelites, or not?' The Lord responded, 'Go, for tomorrow I will give them into your hands.'

Judges 20:28 (NIV)

The story in Judges 20:18–48 used to confuse me. The Israelites asked God for counsel on whether to go to battle. God told them to fight. The Israelites listened, and they lost, suffering 22,000 casualties. The Israelites went back to God to ask for counsel, and the reply was the same. They lost again, suffering another 18,000 casualties. A third time, the Israelites went before God and asked for counsel. God answered, 'Go, for tomorrow I will give them into your hands.' Finally, the Israelites won.

As I read this story, I wondered, *Why would God clearly guide the Israelites and then allow them to fail?* It didn't make sense to me. But this past year, when I faced my own apparent failure after following God's will for me, I saw this beautiful truth: God's ways are not our ways and God's thoughts are not ours.

In each battle, the Israelites were learning the best strategies to prepare them for future battles. And most important, they were learning to have complete faith and dependence on God despite the circumstances. God sees victory even in our apparent defeat because God knows the important lessons we are learning along the way.

Prayer: *Heavenly Father, may our strength in you never falter. And may you continue to finish your perfect work in us. Amen*

Thought for the day: God will use my moments of discouragement to complete a good work in me.

Kayla Reay (Victoria, Australia)

Breathe

Read Psalm 145:13–21

One day Jesus was praying in a certain place. When he finished, one of his disciples said to him, 'Lord, teach us to pray, just as John taught his disciples.'
Luke 11:1 (NIV)

A few years ago, I studied acting. One of the classes taught techniques for breathing and movement. Just prior to the acting sessions, we would lie down on the floor and practise slow and deep breathing exercises. The purpose was to gain coordination as we incorporated the breathing and movement techniques into our acting sessions. It was something relatively simple to do but at times some of us would skip this regimen. That was when the professor would vigorously call out: 'Breathe!' And we would stop what we were doing, lie down, and begin our breathing routine.

I see a similarity in our life of prayer. It can be easy to be distracted by other tasks and fail to nourish our spiritual life with active prayer. Many times we are full of excuses. Communion with God, our Breath of Life, is always free and God wants us to be fully engaged. Prayer is an opportunity to breathe deeply and coordinate heart, mind, body and soul to be attentive to God's voice.

Prayer: *God of creation, centre our thoughts so we can be in complete communion with you. Thank you for teaching us to pray: 'Father, hallowed be your name, your kingdom come. Give us each day our daily bread. Forgive us our sins, for we also forgive everyone who sins against us. And lead us not into temptation' (Luke 11:2–4). Amen*

Thought for the day: Prayer is an opportunity to breathe deeply.

Alan Li Camarillo (Missouri, USA)

Pause and consider

Read Ephesians 4:29–32

All scripture is God-breathed and is useful for teaching, rebuking, correcting and training in righteousness.

2 Timothy 3:16 (NIV)

A friend was visiting, and we read *The Upper Room* together. The passage that day was the parable of the unmerciful servant, and the prayer focus was 'Someone I need to forgive.' We talked about the devotion, but I did not think much about it.

Later that day, we were shopping together when I received a rude message that made me angry. As I was fuming and complaining to my friend, she gently reminded me of what we had read that morning. She urged me to see the other person's side and to let go of my anger and my need to be right. I realised that it is easy to get angry, but my anger does not bring about the righteousness God desires. God gave me the exact words and company I needed that day, even before I knew it.

Sometimes, it is easier to get carried away by our feelings than to pause and consider what God is saying about our situation. We have to make a conscious choice to step back and see the situation in the light of God's word. I hope the next time God speaks to me, I will pause and listen.

Prayer: *Heavenly Father, help us to listen to your promptings through your word and those around us. When we face obstacles, help us to trust you. In Jesus' name. Amen*

Thought for the day: Today I will listen carefully for the ways God is speaking to me.

Jennifer Kingsley (Alabama, USA)

Love your neighbours

Read Micah 6:6–8

What does the Lord require of you? To act justly and to love mercy and to walk humbly with your God.
Micah 6:8 (NIV)

In April 2020, I started cooking food every Wednesday for people in my community who were living on the streets. When I prepare stir-fry, the shallot, ginger and spring onion fill our whole house with good smells. The natural colours of different vegetables – green, red, purple, brown – decorate the dishes and entice my husband to join me in preparing the food. After cutting the roast chicken, he places it into the box, arranging it like a five-star hotel chef would.

This is how we show God's love and share it with others, filling our life with joy and harmony. Everyone wants to be loved. It only takes a small act. When we give a little time, we can help make a big difference in others' lives. People who give also receive happiness and love. When we give to and love each other, we can create a more beautiful world.

Prayer: *O Lord, help us to show your love and mercy to others. Amen*

Thought for the day: Today I will take time to share God's love.

Stella Ting (Hong Kong, China)

Burden bearers

Read Exodus 28:15–30

'Whenever Aaron enters the Holy Place, he will bear the names of the sons of Israel over his heart on the breastpiece of decision.'
Exodus 28:29 (NIV)

The high priest of the Old Testament gives us a beautiful picture of bearing burdens. He has chains running over his shoulders to enable him to carry the breastpiece which covers his heart. The breastpiece was made of gold and had twelve precious stones set into it, each engraved with the name of one of the tribes of Israel. Worn together with the gold ephod, it would have been heavy. Symbolically the high priest was carrying the burden of the twelve tribes of Israel into God's presence.

We may often feel burdened for family or friends and sometimes distant peoples who are suffering grievously. What can we do to help? We can take these needy ones as precious jewels and carry them on our hearts. Sometimes they are heavy and we feel weighed down, but I remember the elderly preacher who, burdened by the message God had laid on his heart, told us: 'When God lays a burden on us, it is a gracious gentle burden.' As Jesus said: 'My yoke is easy and my burden is light' (Matthew 11:30).

It is a long time since I was able to carry even the lightest burden on my shoulder, but I thank God that, like the high priest of ancient Israel, I am able to be a burden bearer for him.

Prayer: *Dear Lord, when we are burdened and concerned for the needs of others, help us to remember that we are yoked together with you, and that you care so much more than we do. Amen*

Thought for the day: I have the privilege of carrying my burdens into the very presence of God.

Pauline Lewis (Wales, United Kingdom)

Bigger than our fears

Read Matthew 6:25–34

'Peace I leave with you; my peace I give you. I do not give to you as the world gives. Do not let your hearts be troubled and do not be afraid.'
John 14:27 (NIV)

Since I was a kid, I have been a worrier. It started with small worries about who I was going to talk to at lunch or who would allow me to join their game at recess. It grew into intense anxiety about almost any social situation. My anxiety was rooted in deep fears about not belonging and facing rejection. These fears clouded most of middle school and high school as I worried that people I considered 'cool' were secretly judging my every action. I did my best to put on a happy face each day, but on the inside I was sinking.

When I opened up to my parents about the roots of my anxiety, they encouraged me to think about where my strength and peace comes from. I realised that I was looking for peace in other people's approval instead of from the one true God. Thus began the slow journey of retraining my brain. Now, when an anxious thought arises, I combat it with scripture and reason instead of letting it take root. Learning to do this takes patience, and the journey never ends. While I am in a much better place than I was two years ago, I still struggle every day. But I know God has provided me with all the tools I need.

Prayer: *Heavenly Father, thank you for giving us minds to think, to be creative and to worship you. In times of mental distress, remind us that you are looking out for us. Amen*

Thought for the day: God is bigger than my fears.

Madison Brown (Texas, USA)

The best gift

Read Ephesians 6:1–4

Start children off on the way they should go, and even when they are old they will not turn from it.
Proverbs 22:6 (NIV)

My father was devoted to God. He taught me how to pray, to evangelise and to have discipline. I am grateful for the ways God used my dad as a vessel to help me in my Christian life. Now that my dad is gone, I have been following in his footsteps and honouring the legacy he left for me by the grace of God.

Over the years, I have been evangelising and disciplining my life each day to the glory of our Saviour Jesus Christ. The time I spend praying, evangelising, reading *The Upper Room* daily devotions, and studying the word of God blesses my life. This time also leads me to better understand God's will, purpose and instructions for my life. No matter what challenges or predicaments I face, I can find solace in God.

What an amazing gift it is for a parent to train his child in the ways of God! This instruction will order the path and brighten the talents, vision and future of a child. Our God would be happy.

Prayer: *Dear God, grant us the wisdom to train our children in your ways. In the name of Jesus. Amen*

Thought for the day: Today I will thank those who have taught me to pray.

Onyema Ndubuisi (Abia, Nigeria)

The end

Read Habakkuk 3:16–19

We are children of God, and what we will be has not yet been made known. But we know that when Christ appears, we shall be like him, for we shall see him as he is.
1 John 3:2 (NIV)

My sister always flips to the back of a new book to see how the story will end. Not me. I love entering into the world of the characters and joining them on their journeys. I have no interest in knowing how things will end ahead of time.

I can't say the same for my own life. I'd love a peek at my future. Soon my last child will reach adulthood. For years being a mum has given me purpose. What will happen when that role ends?

The book of Habakkuk gives me comfort. Habakkuk laments the violence and destruction that surrounds him. His situation doesn't change, yet, by the end of the book, he is rejoicing. What made the difference? God tells him how the story ends. I imagine God saying, 'Don't worry, Habakkuk. I've got this. It's going to be okay.' Knowing God's plans for the future renewed Habakkuk's faith in God's sovereignty in the present. Confusion and fear lost their grip on his heart.

I may not know what my life will look like in a few years, but, as in Habakkuk's case, God has shown me how things will end. One day, I will be remade in the likeness of Christ and will live with him forever. Now that's worth flipping to the end.

Prayer: *Dear God, thank you for revealing to us the glorious end. Help us to trust in your good plans for our lives. Amen*

Thought for the day: In times of uncertainty, I will entrust my future to God.

Laura Kuehn (Connecticut, USA)

Kaleidoscope

Read 1 Corinthians 12:4–11

By the word of the Lord the heavens were made, their starry host by the breath of his mouth.
Psalm 33:6 (NIV)

A kaleidoscope is a tube-shaped toy containing mirrors and coloured pieces. A person looks into one end of the tube and turns it to view constantly changing patterns. I started collecting these toys over 40 years ago because I was fascinated by the seemingly endless variety of designs they created.

Over the years I began to realise that the universe itself is much like a kaleidoscope. We can look at the sky to view an ever-changing panorama. God created a vast array of plants, animals, rocks and people, where there are seldom two exactly alike. How boring it would be if everything were the same! God has gifted us with a vast universe of diverse creations for our pleasure and God's glory.

Prayer: *Creator God, help us to appreciate diversity in nature and in the people we meet. We pray as your Son taught us, 'Our Father which art in heaven, Hallowed be thy name. Thy kingdom come. Thy will be done in earth, as it is in heaven. Give us this day our daily bread. And forgive us our debts, as we forgive our debtors. And lead us not into temptation, but deliver us from evil: For thine is the kingdom, and the power, and the glory, for ever' (Matthew 6:9–13, KJV). Amen*

Thought for the day: I will appreciate the rich diversity of God's universe every day.

Michael Joseph Hotchkiss (Virginia, USA)

God is good

Read Psalm 29
The Lord gives strength to his people; the Lord blesses his people with peace.
Psalm 29:11 (NIV)

Since childhood I have been a good student, an active participant in church activities and part of a well-known family in my community. Being the best and succeeding in the eyes of others was an ambition of mine – until I experienced failure.

I failed the entrance exam for my dream college, despite studying hard. Good relations in my family broke down. Although I worked hard, I was unable to accomplish my dream of studying abroad. Despite being known as active and smart in college, I didn't get a job that others considered good. At 27 years old, I was not married, I often worried excessively about the future and I was diagnosed with a mental disorder that often interferes with my relationships.

Experiencing these disappointments sent me into a deep depression because I felt unable and unprepared to face them. I am grateful that Jesus Christ reminded me that I will always be strengthened through prayer, God's word and the people who support me. I believe that God is sovereign and always good, no matter what my situation is. Even when I fail, God loves me and often teaches me through failure. And God's presence and love offer comfort and give me strength.

Prayer: *Loving Father God, teach us to be grateful for our experiences and to believe that you are always good, no matter our circumstances. Amen*

Thought for the day: Even when I fail, I will be grateful to God.

Berthin Sappang (East Kalimantan, Indonesia)

PRAYER FOCUS: PEOPLE SUFFERING FROM DEPRESSION

Helping Jesus

Read Deuteronomy 11:18–20

'Watch and pray so that you will not fall into temptation. The spirit is willing, but the flesh is weak.'
Matthew 26:41 (NIV)

Most of us can remember 'helping' our parents when we were children. For me, helping usually consisted of my holding a tool while my father worked nearby. Sometimes I'd get to turn a wrench or finish pounding a nail, but my father could easily have done those tasks without me. Eventually I realised that this time spent helping my father was an opportunity for me to learn and practise skills that I would one day teach my children.

I think that Jesus was doing the same thing with his disciples in Gethsemane. 'Watch and pray,' Jesus says to them after they've fallen asleep, 'so you don't fall into temptation.' Jesus is not asking them to do this for his own benefit but for theirs.

Just as my father used my help to teach me the things I would need to know as I grew into adulthood, God invites us to participate in serving the world. Whether through prayer and worship, caring for the poor, looking out for those who are alone or providing for those without housing, God uses these opportunities to shape us into mature disciples.

God includes us not because the job can't be done without our help but because God has chosen to involve all of us in the work of the kingdom.

Prayer: *Almighty God, thank you for involving us in your work in the world. Help us to see opportunities each day to love you and serve our neighbours. Amen*

Thought for the day: Every circumstance is an opportunity to learn how to serve God.

Jason Koon (North Carolina, USA)

A new man

Read 2 Corinthians 5:16–21

If any man be in Christ, he is a new creature.
2 Corinthians 5:17 (KJV)

In spring 2009 I hit rock bottom. Many times in my years of alcohol and drug abuse I thought that I had reached my lowest point, but they paled in comparison. This time I found myself in a tiny jail cell with no one left to turn to. With nothing to lose, I sank to my knees and prayed in total desperation. I begged God to forgive me for the way I had lived my life and asked God to show me a better way.

Soon after that prayer, God's love became real for me. I received treatment I had desperately needed for years and finally was delivered from the desire to use alcohol and drugs. People I had hurt despite their love for me began to return to my life. God started to open new doors for me, and I was able to see how I could use my experiences to help others who were suffering as I once had.

Today I am a new man in Christ. Although I am still serving time for crimes I committed while on drugs, my relationship with God is unwavering. I go to God each day, asking God to use me as a vessel of divine love. Through me God has been able to change lives. I remain a witness to God's amazing grace.

Prayer: *For your forgiveness, my God, I thank you. For the new life you are always ready to give, I thank you. For your love that never leaves me alone, I thank you. Amen*

Thought for the day: When I have hit rock bottom, God's love can lift me up.

Christopher King (Delaware, USA)

Two strangers

Read Luke 10:25–29

'Who is my neighbour?'
Luke 10:29 (NIV)

I attended an inspiring conference in Gothenburg, Sweden, some years ago. Many of the speakers were focused on the importance of knowing our neighbours. After the conference was over, I planned to take the bus back home to Sarpsborg in Norway. When the bus was delayed, I sat outside in the sunshine, reading a book.

A young woman approached and asked those around me if they had any small change for her. Most people declined. *Did I have any Swedish money left?* I thought. The woman passed me slowly as I greeted her and gave her 20 Swedish krona (about £1.50), which was all I had. She thanked me, and I touched her arm gently. 'God bless you,' I said. 'May the Lord bless you as well,' she answered. I became braver: 'May I mention you in my prayers? What is your name?' 'Belinda,' she said. 'I used to pray, but now I find it difficult. Would you pray for me and my little girl that the child welfare office has taken from me? Her name is Lina.' I rose from where I sat and hugged her.

From that bus station encounter in Gothenburg, two strangers became my neighbours. Since that day I have been praying for Belinda and Lina. And I know that God hears my prayers. After all, it was God who made them known to me.

Prayer: *Dear Lord, thank you for letting us into your heart. May your love and grace go with us every step of our lives. We pray in the name of Jesus. Amen*

Thought for the day: God knows no borders.

Gerd Helene Rosok (Norway)

Listen

Read Mark 9:2–13

A cloud appeared and covered them, and a voice came from the cloud: 'This is my Son, whom I love. Listen to him!'
Mark 9:7 (NIV)

Our flight attendant was getting frustrated. She was explaining the emergency safety procedures, but many of us were either ignoring her or engaged in other conversations. Eventually she raised her voice and authoritatively declared, 'Listen up! This could save your life!' Her command surprised and embarrassed me. But it got my attention, and I began listening as though my life depended on it.

Peter, James and John had surely made assumptions about who Jesus was and what he meant to them that limited their ability to listen to him afresh. But Jesus shook them free of these assumptions with the transfiguration.

My own assumptions around scripture often keep me from hearing what might be life-changing truth. I assume I already know the message when I encounter familiar scriptures, and my mind tends to wander when I hear unfamiliar words. Every Sunday, the minister invites us to 'listen for the word of God,' but I confess that I do not always listen afresh. However, I can heed the words of the flight attendant who once exposed my cavalier attitude and learn to listen to God's word as though my life depends on it. Surely it does.

Prayer: *Dear Lord, open our ears that we may hear your words of truth for our lives. Amen*

Thought for the day: Today I will listen to scripture as though my life depends on what I hear.

William G. Heck (North Carolina, USA)

Never-failing love

Read Matthew 5:43–48

'He makes his sun rise on the evil and on the good and sends rain on the righteous and on the unrighteous.'
Matthew 5:45 (NRSV)

We had just planted a few vegetable seedlings when our town had continuous cold and rainy days for a week. Tender sprouts of green beans were just peeking out of the ground. But because of the cold weather, nothing showed any sign of further growth. Sadly, some leaves were even curling up due to the cold spell in the middle of spring. I was concerned about my garden. Would it survive without the warmth of the sun?

As I looked out one morning, the sun was shining and the birds were singing! *Surely, the day looks different*, I thought. I stepped out to see how it felt outdoors. What a nice warm day! I felt good. When I looked at the plants in my garden they seemed to feel good, too. What a difference the sun had made!

The warmth of the sun made me realise my gratitude to God, whose warmth embraces me in all weather and circumstances. What's more amazing is that God's rain and sun benefit all people, whether they are righteous or unrighteous. I also remembered the faith of the displaced Israelites, who affirmed, 'The steadfast love of the Lord never ceases, his mercies never come to an end; they are new every morning' (Lamentations 3:22–23). Let us give thanks for God's never-failing love.

Prayer: *Loving God, we receive your gifts with joy. We are grateful that your blessings are assured for us always. Amen*

Thought for the day: God's gifts never cease.

Paul Benjamin (New Jersey, USA)

Finding God

Read Job 42:1–6
Come near to God and he will come near to you.
James 4:8 (NIV)

The year 2019 was a turning point for me, as well as one of the lowest times in my life. My husband and I lost our first child, who was only four days old. I struggled to accept and understand why such a good and loving God would allow all this to happen. Often I have questions, and there are no satisfactory answers.

I thought that believers would be blessed and spared from suffering and difficulties. But God helped me understand that all people experience suffering; there are no exceptions. God brought to my mind the story of Job, who was faithful and godly, but who suffered greatly. And even Jesus experienced great suffering on the cross.

Through my suffering, I realised that I didn't have complete control over my life. Because of that, suffering could make people reject God. But at the same time, suffering leads us to a deeper knowledge of God. God longs for us to draw near and will enter into our suffering with us so that we may overcome.

Prayer: *Dear God, help us to find you amid our suffering. Draw us closer to you. Amen*

Thought for the day: How has my suffering led me closer to God?

Paramytha Magdalena Sukarno Putri (East Java, Indonesia)

PRAYER FOCUS: PARENTS GRIEVING THE LOSS OF A CHILD

God's Spirit intercedes

Read Romans 8:26–28

The Spirit comes to help our weakness. We don't know what we should pray, but the Spirit himself pleads our case with unexpressed groans.
Romans 8:26 (CEB)

My wife and I developed the habit of praying together before bed each night. Typically, I pray aloud for our marriage, our children, friends, church and community, and for other concerns of the day, while my wife prays silently. We have learned that time together in prayer is powerful.

Recently, after a gruelling week at work, finding words for prayer was a struggle. I couldn't articulate my own needs or vocalise my hurt and pain. I managed a few words and an 'Amen,' but just then my wife broke her normal silence. She spoke to my deepest need with a prayer for God to equip me with renewed confidence and courage. Her prayer captured what I had been struggling with – courage to stand up for myself and my family, and confidence to believe in my value, worth and abilities at home and work.

As I reflected on the weight of both her words and the Spirit's inspiration, I thought of today's scripture reading and took courage. Even when our words are muffled and muddled by pain too hard to express, the Spirit intercedes for us before God.

Prayer: *Gracious God, when we struggle to pray, remind us that you intercede for us. Thank you for surrounding us with a community that gives voice to our needs and prays on our behalf. Amen*

Thought for the day: When I cannot pray, the Holy Spirit prays for me.

Cassius Rhue (South Carolina, USA)

God's constant watch

Read Psalm 121

No! Israel's protector never sleeps or rests!
Psalm 121:4 (CEB)

As a child, I was sometimes plagued by vivid nightmares. Once when I was eight or nine, I awoke terrified though I could not remember what had frightened me. It was still fairly early in the evening, but I had been asleep for some time and was quite disoriented. I stumbled to my bedroom door. When I opened it, I could see down the hall into our living room. My father was still awake, sitting quietly in his chair reading the newspaper.

Even now, decades later, I remember the feeling of peace that came over me seeing my father there. He didn't notice me, but his presence reminded me of the many times he had protected and calmed me in the past. Based on this history of faithfulness and love, I knew that I was safe. I quietly went back to bed and quickly fell asleep.

When I think back on that moment, I'm reminded that our God never sleeps. God is always aware of us. God knows our needs and stands ready to come to our aid. We are never far from God. That is truly a reason for peace.

Prayer: *Ever-vigilant God, thank you for your constant care and protection. In times of trouble, help us to remember your faithfulness. Amen*

Thought for the day: God is never far from me.

Lisa Stackpole (Wisconsin, USA)

Letting God define me

Read Zechariah 2:1–5

'Jerusalem will be a city without walls because of the great number of people and animals in it. And I myself will be a wall of fire around it,' declares the Lord, 'and I will be its glory within.'
Zechariah 2:4–5 (NIV)

I first read today's scripture passage when I was in college. At the time, I was trying to figure out what I was doing with my life. All these years later, that question has not entirely gone away. We live in a world of checking boxes; clarity of purpose, achievements and attainable goals hold a lot of weight. Those things have their purpose. It's good to be intentional about what we do and how we do it. However, this verse challenged me – and continues to challenge me – to let go of my desire for security and my need to be in control.

As scary as letting go may be, this challenge comes with a promise that far exceeds its demands. When I don't build defensive walls to make myself feel safe, when I don't try to measure and control what is within me, I am free to give myself to God. God does more with our lives than we can ask, hope or imagine. We trade in the security of human walls to accept in faith that God will be a wall of fire around us. We trade in the measurements of worldly accomplishments to give God space to be the glory within.

Prayer: *Heavenly Father, help us to let go of our desire for control and to rest in the knowledge that you take care of us better than we can take care of ourselves. Amen*

Thought for the day: I will rejoice in the freedom of surrendering my life to God.

Máire Íde Ní hÁgain (Northern Ireland, United Kingdom)

We shall be changed

The year 2010 is marked with personal historical significance. I witnessed my mother move from diagnosis to death in under a month. While I was blessed to spend the last three weeks of her life by her side in the hospital, that did not prepare me for the sheer heartbreak I felt when she died. I remember very little of the outdoor burial — the gathering of friends and family far and wide under an overcast canopy of clouds. It all seemed surreal to me. But that same year, I witnessed the birth of my best friend's grandson. Nothing in my life had prepared me for the intensity of labour — the pain, the fragility and the exuberance of watching a child come into the world. There I was, humbled by life and death in the same year. Two new gray hairs just above my left ear were proof that my nervous system had been devastated by the ultimate — life and death.

I imagine the coming of the Holy Spirit at Pentecost was similarly intense — violent winds, tongues of fire, the curious fluidity of speech and understanding. One Bible translation reports that those who witnessed the Spirit that day were amazed and astonished. I imagine them humbled and devasted by the ultimate. In this case, the ultimate was a manifestation of the Spirit of God. The crowd who had gathered sensed something just out of reach — the letting go of the familiar to embrace the unknown. They asked bewildered, 'How is it that we hear, each of us, in our own native language?' (Acts 2:8, NRSV). The people gathered witnessed something Howard Thurman in *Meditations of the Heart* (Beacon Press, 1953) refers to as 'the growing edge'. Thurman writes profoundly about the birthing and dying of things all around us. He writes, 'Look well to the growing edge. All around us worlds are dying and new worlds are being born.'

There are multiple ways to respond to that which we have no control over. The crowds who experienced Pentecost had mixed reactions. Some marvelled; others questioned; still others sneered. How easy it is to dismiss the unfamiliar, to sneer at what we do not understand – even those of us who are religious, compelled by mystery and attuned to the profound. How easy it is to forget the liberty at which the Spirit of

God can enter all the spaces of our lives. At Pentecost, the arrival of the Spirit is so monumental that it marks a new era of time, a new epoch, an announcement of what to expect in these 'last days'.

Luckily Peter is there to address the crowd, to lessen their overwhelm, and to guide them into time and timelessness, the promise of salvation for them and their children and 'for all who are far away' (Acts 2:39). Peter's message is just right for an imbalanced world that operates more on what it can measure, interrogate, evaluate and project on to. The message Peter preaches is a caution to us that we belong to a world that is not always discernible, a world that cannot always be manipulated. The text he reads cautions us that hierarchical relationships will cease. The distinction in gifts of the Spirit will cease. Preaching, prophetic dreams, revelation — these gifts of the Spirit will fall upon *all flesh*. Even nature shall participate in the unexpected and the out-of-the-ordinary. In a word, Peter is describing the kingdom of God come near. We cannot exactly anticipate what that will mean for each of us. But we shall be changed. In social terms, it might mean that our divisions shall cease. In political terms, it might mean that our corruptions shall fall away. In spiritual terms, it might mean that our devotion shall go unquenched. But whatever it means, we shall find ourselves caught up in the humbling power of the Holy, who will ultimately perfect our love and invite us to be changed.

QUESTIONS FOR REFLECTION

1 Recall a time when a disruption gave you a clearer awareness of God's presence. What was the disruption? What did you learn about God from that experience?

2 Which of your routines have become more important than the purpose they were intended to serve?

3 How will you disrupt one of your routines to make room for the Holy Spirit to push you in a new direction?

Lindsay L. Gray, editorial director

A way in the wilderness

Read Isaiah 43:14–21

I am about to do a new thing; now it springs forth; do you not perceive it? I will make a way in the wilderness and rivers in the desert.
Isaiah 43:19 (NRSV)

Some years ago, I was in a financial wilderness. I had no way of earning money, and my greatest need was food. The Lord promised to make a way in the wilderness and rivers in the desert for the Israelites, and I trusted that if I could somehow get food for my family, the Lord would provide for my other needs in time.

I didn't know where I would get money for food. But then someone unexpectedly gave me a piece of land for cultivation. I planted maize and beans and experienced an abundant yield. God had indeed made a way in the wilderness.

We will all enter a wilderness at some point – financial crisis, sickness, isolation. But God will always make a way. Sometimes it may seem miraculous: the provision of a well-paying job, new and successful business ventures, healing. But other times, God works in simple ways like making a part-time job available to us or sending someone to keep us company when we are lonely. We can trust God to make a way for us in every wilderness.

Prayer: *Dear God, help us trust you to get us through every hard situation we face. In Jesus' name. Amen*

Thought for the day: God will make a way in every situation.

Enid Adah Nyinomujuni (Dar es Salaam, Tanzania)

Seeking God

Read Jeremiah 29:10–14

*'You will seek me and find me when you seek me with all your heart.
I will be found by you,' declares the Lord.*
Jeremiah 29:13–14 (NIV)

It was one of the most precious gifts my husband ever gave me. The 18 fuzzy, day-old chicks toddled to and fro exploring their new home. They sipped water, nibbled feed and snuggled together under the heat lamp. Caring for chicks was a new experience for me. I checked on them throughout the day.

Each time I came near, one chick would race over to me and then jump up and down. I wasn't sure what she was doing, but one day I decided to pick her up. She calmed down and sat quietly in my hands. It delighted my heart that she wanted me more than the things I had provided. While the other chicks wobbled to the food, water and warmth, she wobbled to me. She grew into a fine hen, beautiful and gentle, and she continued to search for me in the farmyard. She would tap my boot with her beak, and I would bend down to see her with great delight.

God used that little chick to show me the wonder of drawing near. Just as she would seek me and find me, we are assured that we can seek and find God. God sees us wobbling and flapping. God feels us tapping and jumping for attention. When we seek God with all our hearts, God lovingly bends down and, with great delight, draws us close.

Prayer: *Dear heavenly Father, thank you for using your creation to give us glimpses of yourself. Help us to seek you with all our hearts. In Jesus' name. Amen*

Thought for the day: Today I will seek God with all my heart.

A. B. Barber (Ohio, USA)

Stepping out in faith

Read Matthew 10:37–42

'The Lord himself goes before you and will be with you; he will never leave you nor forsake you. Do not be afraid; do not be discouraged.'
Deuteronomy 31:8 (NIV)

I wiped my tears as I hurried to my car after leaving the senior-care facility where my mother lived. She was 89 years old and had dementia. My heart was aching after saying goodbye; I didn't know when I'd see her again. My husband was an Anglican priest and had accepted a call to serve in a parish almost five hours away. I would no longer be able to visit my mum every day as I'd done for the past few years.

I loved my mother so much it hurt. Although she no longer spoke, she still recognised me when I visited. Her eyes lit up when she saw me, and she would touch my hair and adjust my scarf or necklace. I worried she wouldn't get the same care without me around, and I was afraid she would forget me.

Walking away from my mother to serve the Lord was a sacrifice. It took courage, faith and a deep trust in God's promises never to leave me or her. Even when we cannot be present to care for our loved ones, God's presence holds our loved ones and doesn't let go. In response, we can step out in faith. We can entrust them to God's care and have confidence that God will strengthen us for our journey.

Prayer: *Dear God, thank you for caring for us and our loved ones. Give us strength to follow your call and serve you. Amen*

Thought for the day: When God calls me to serve, I will trust God's promises and follow.

Nancy Robinson (New Brunswick, Canada)

Beautiful vessels

Read John 4:7–14

Jesus stood and said in a loud voice, 'Let anyone who is thirsty come to me and drink. Whoever believes in me, as Scripture has said, rivers of living water will flow from within them.' By this he meant the Spirit.
John 7:37–39 (NIV)

When my children were young, I showed them an interesting experiment I had heard about. I cut a few wildflowers called Queen Anne's lace and placed several of them in three different glasses of water. I left one glass with clear water, added a few drops of red food colouring to the second glass and a few drops of blue food colouring to the third. The next morning the flowers in the clear water were still their original white colour, but the ones in the red water had turned red and the ones in the blue water had turned blue.

Just as the water is drawn into the flowers, we need to draw Christ's living water in our lives. As the Holy Spirit flows into us, we are changed and empowered to be more Christlike, to do the will of God just as Jesus did. The Spirit can change us to be beautiful vessels of honour for God. As we continue to draw that living water of the Holy Spirit into our hearts through Bible study and prayer, we continue to grow in Christlike beauty.

Prayer: *Dear Jesus, we pray for your living water to make us more like you each day. Amen*

Thought for the day: The Holy Spirit helps me grow in Christlike beauty.

Hank DeGraaff (Michigan, USA)

A second chance

Read James 2:14–17

Listen, my dear brothers and sisters: has not God chosen those who are poor in the eyes of the world to be rich in faith and to inherit the kingdom he promised those who love him?
James 2:5 (NIV)

It was a busy day, and I was at my church trying to fix a dripping tap. I discovered I needed to replace a gasket, so I drove to the hardware store. As I entered the parking lot, I saw a man sitting on the curb holding a sign that said, 'Hungry – Please Help.' I had traffic behind me and I was in a hurry, so I didn't stop. As I left the parking lot, I saw the man again but still didn't stop.

Driving back to the church, I kept thinking about that man, and I felt compelled to go back and give him some money. But when I returned, the man was not there. Looking around, I noticed an old, battered truck. The man I had seen holding the sign was inside, so I pulled over, rolled down the window and asked him to come over – which he did. I gave him some money and wished him well. He thanked me, and I left.

As I left the parking lot, replaying what had happened, I was overcome with emotion. Surely it was God who had gotten my attention and encouraged me to help that man. I thanked God for this second chance and asked God to help me to be more attentive and responsive to those in need in the future.

Prayer: *Loving Father, help us be more aware of those in need around us, and give us the desire and the courage to respond with compassion. In Jesus' name. Amen*

Thought for the day: Opportunities to help those in need are all around me.

Byron S. Wills (Oregon, USA)

Lost

Read Isaiah 30:19–21

When you turn to the right or when you turn to the left, your ears shall hear a word behind you, saying, 'This is the way; walk in it.'
Isaiah 30:21 (NRSV)

Whether navigating through hospital corridors or driving down country roads, I am easily disoriented. I usually end up making a wrong turn or two and have to turn around. Part of the problem is that I am easily distracted and don't pay attention to the landmarks and signs posted along the way.

Sometimes our spiritual journey is like this. We may become distracted and miss the guidance God gives us. When we're lost, we can find our way back to God by purposefully seeking God and listening for God's guidance.

When we read and meditate on God's word, pray and worship, we are more attuned to God's gentle promptings. Regular fellowship with other believers also helps us stay focused on God. The prophet Isaiah reminds us that we will hear a word guiding our steps when we make a conscious effort to listen to God. Even when we feel disconnected from God, we can find peace in the promise that God is waiting and will guide our steps.

Prayer: *Dear God, thank you for being our gentle shepherd who promises to lead us and guide us always. We pray as Jesus taught us, 'Father, hallowed be your name, your kingdom come. Give us each day our daily bread. Forgive us our sins, for we also forgive everyone who sins against us. And lead us not into temptation' (Luke 11:2–4, NIV). Amen*

Thought for the day: I will purposefully listen for God's guidance today.

Melanie S. Fretz (Pennsylvania, USA)

Jesus shows us the way

Read Psalm 32

Why do you see the speck in your neighbour's eye but do not notice the log in your own eye?
Luke 6:41 (NRSV)

I had returned to college in early September after a trip home, and I was walking towards the college hostel from the bus stop. Some construction had begun while we were on vacation, and many holes had been dug on the side of the road. While I was walking, I spotted a boy talking on his mobile phone. He was absorbed in his conversation and seemed unconcerned about the dangers on the road. I reprimanded him in my heart and watched every step he took, expecting him to fall into a hole at any time. I kept my eyes fixed on the boy as I wondered, *If he falls, should I pull him out of the hole and then scold him for his carelessness or should I scold him first and then pull him out?* As I was choosing my words and deciding how harsh I should be, I stopped paying attention to my path and fell into a hole.

I realised then that looking at the faults of others can cause us to stumble. I prayed that day for Jesus to show me the right path in my life. The psalmist proclaims that God will protect and deliver us. We always can rely on God to show us the way.

Prayer: *Forgiving God, help us listen to you and to walk in the right path. Amen*

Thought for the day: If I pay attention, God will show me the way.

M. Ramki (Sri Lanka)

God sightings

Read 1 Kings 19:9–16

After the earthquake came a fire, but the Lord was not in the fire. And after the fire came a gentle whisper.

1 Kings 19:12 (NIV)

When I was in college, I went to Mexico on a mission trip. Every evening after working at different building sites, teaching vacation Bible school and interacting with the local community, our group would gather for worship. We took some time to share what we called 'God sightings'. Where did we see God that day? How did we see God show up in the interactions we had? We were encouraged to share even the smallest experience.

As people started to share, it would spark memories for other people. We looked for ways God was showing up in small moments, and we always found God.

Often we look for God to move in mighty ways. We look for the parting of the sea, but we forget that so many times, God shows up in the simple moments, guiding our steps each day. In each small need that is met, we are reminded that God is with us in something as simple as a sunrise or a smile from a stranger.

When we take the time to be aware of all that God is doing, we will see God more often. Each time we see God in the world is an opportunity to offer praise and to connect with our loving creator.

Prayer: *Dear God, help us to see you in the small, ordinary moments of our lives. Amen*

Thought for the day: God is present in the big and small moments of my life.

Tynea Lewis (Pennsylvania, USA)

Lesson of love

Read Matthew 19:13–15

Jesus said, 'Let the little children come to me, and do not hinder them, for the kingdom of heaven belongs to such as these.'
Matthew 19:14 (NIV)

I teach a series of classes designed to help children learn how Jesus' interactions with people transformed them. Towards the end of the semester, we schedule a class visit to a residential community centre for adults. Ahead of time, we hold special sessions with the children to prepare them for the visit. Prior to one such visit, I noticed a few children who showed no interest at all. I felt sad thinking our visit might not go well.

On the day of our visit to the centre, I was greatly surprised to find the children enthusiastic. They had on their best clothes, had brought homemade snacks prepared especially for the occasion, and were ready to show off their musical talents. Once at the centre, the children's eyes were wide with expectation. They shared smiles, games, laughter and hugs.

Later, when we evaluated the visit, everyone had something positive to share. There is no doubt that the shared experience at the centre was the work of the Lord. On that visit, my students and I learned that the love of God is boundless and that the Holy Spirit surprises us at every turn.

Prayer: *Dear God, thank you for your infinite love. Please hold especially close to you those who feel unloved or forgotten. Amen*

Thought for the day: God's love is boundless.

Sandra R. dos Santos (Montevideo, Uruguay)

In the night

Read Psalm 4

Return, O my soul, to your rest, for the Lord has dealt bountifully with you.
Psalm 116:7 (NRSV)

I was going through a difficult time, and I had a lot on my mind. Unfortunately, my sleep was affected by the stress, and the resulting fatigue severely impaired my daily functioning. Eventually I realised I couldn't handle it on my own, and I asked God for assistance.

Soon I adopted a new routine. When I awakened at night, I would spend ten minutes at my desk praying, writing down my concerns and putting them in God's hands. If my concerns seemed trivial, I would conclude, 'Quiet your mind. Everything's fine.' If the worries were more significant, I would tell myself, 'Quiet your mind. God's at your side.' When I went back to bed, I would recite comforting Bible verses. I put all of my worries in God's hands and would usually drift peacefully back to sleep.

I intend to keep my night times with God. As the psalmist says: 'I will bless the Lord who advises me; even at night I am instructed in the depths of my mind' (Psalm 16:7, CEB). God not only comforts me; God gives me wisdom at night.

Prayer: *Dear Lord, comfort us in the night as well as in the day. Help us to turn all our worries over to you. Amen*

Thought for the day: All day and all night, God is by my side.

Bruce Bedingfield (Illinois, USA)

The place for lament

Read Lamentations 1:1–7
How deserted lies the city, once so full of people!
Lamentations 1:1 (NIV)

Lamentations is a heartbreaking commentary on the state of Jerusalem after it fell to the Babylonians. Few people remained in the shattered city; the rest had died or gone into exile and had no one to comfort them.

I felt some of this pain when my church split. After so many people left our church in the city to start a new one in the suburbs, I was heartbroken. I looked around our historic sanctuary, its stained-glass windows shining over vacant pews. Our empty Sunday school hall echoed; with more teachers than children, it was all too quiet. It felt like God was no longer with us either; I was tempted to despair. Just as the grieving prophet of Lamentations remembered his beautiful city, I thought back on services filled with smiling people, children singing and banners waving.

Lamentations offers us a map through grief. First, reality is faced boldly and loss felt bravely. Then that searing pain is brought to God. The prophet who wrote the book cries out, 'See, Lord, how distressed I am! I am in torment within' (Lamentations 1:20). Only then can he move on to hope; only then can the rebuilding start. It is the same with me. When something terrible happens, I cannot fully heal until I face reality, pour out my pain and lean into God's presence – even when God feels far away.

Prayer: *Almighty God, help us to bring our pain and sorrow to you. Give us the courage to lament our losses and tell you how we really feel. Amen*

Thought for the day: God is big enough to bear my grief.

Colleen Scheid (Ohio, USA)

Selah

Read Psalm 3

I cried unto the Lord with my voice, and he heard me out of his holy hill. Selah.
Psalm 3:4 (KJV)

In January 2021, I lost my primary job. My salary from that job paid for my family's daily needs. I had another job, but the salary was not paid monthly. I was stressed, and I found it difficult to find a new job.

In times of stress I remember the word *Selah*, which appears often in the Psalms. In Psalm 3, David has fled from his son Absalom. Though scholars do not know the exact meaning of *Selah*, I wonder if David included it to mean 'take a breath' or 'pause and reflect' on the meaning of the words. After David sang, 'I cried unto the Lord with my voice, and he heard me out of his holy hill,' I wonder if he stopped singing and said to himself, *Do not worry, God will give you deliverance*. When I was stressed over losing my job, I felt that God gave me *Selah* to help me remember that rather than worrying I can pray, praise and worship God.

The word *Selah* in Psalm 3 does not mean the singing is finished. After *Selah*, David once again began praising God. When I am stressed, I remember to pause and then continue praising God, trusting that God cares for me and hears my prayers.

Prayer: *Dear God, in times of hardship, allow us to rest in your steadfast love and mercy. Amen*

Thought for the day: Today I will take a moment to pause and praise God.

Linawati Santoso (East Java, Indonesia)

God knows

Read Luke 8:40–48

Neither death nor life… nor anything else in all creation, will be able to separate us from the love of God that is in Christ Jesus our Lord.
Romans 8:38–39 (NIV)

It's an emergency. A little girl lay dying. Jesus is on his way. In the crowd is a woman who has been unwell for twelve years. She shouldn't be there, as the law forbids her to have contact with others because she is 'unclean' due to menstrual illness. But she is desperate, exhausted and at her wits end, having tried every conceivable means of healing. Her only hope is Jesus. There won't be another opportunity to approach Jesus, but she wants to go unnoticed, so she reaches out and touches Jesus' cloak for healing. And it happens!

But then Jesus stops in his tracks and calls her out. He interrupts his urgent schedule for the woman. She has risked everything by being in the crowd, and Jesus perceives just how incredibly needy she is. He stops, recognising the unspoken dire state of a woman without hope and on the margins of society. He knows all about her. In healing the woman, he enables her to be restored to the community, to family and to God.

I, too, cannot hide from God. He knows all about me. It's no use pretending. He sees my deepest needs, but he doesn't turn away when I reach out to him, even when I can't express my concerns and struggles. And I learn that just as I am I can come to God and receive his forgiveness and transforming grace.

Prayer: *Father, we reach out for you today, thankful that you know and meet our every need. Amen*

Thought for the day: God knows everything about me.

Hilary Allen (England, United Kingdom)

Wonderfully made

Read Psalm 139:1–14

I will praise thee; for I am fearfully and wonderfully made: marvellous are thy works; and that my soul knoweth right well.
Psalm 139:14 (KJV)

I have challenges with learning and social interaction. It may take me hours to complete a 20-minute project. I don't always comprehend what I am reading right away, and I struggle with communicating in social settings. I have lived in fear and anxiety, afraid that my difficulties would be discovered, making me vulnerable to embarrassment and others' laughter.

In today's scripture the psalmist honours and exalts God for the way God made him, calling God's works 'marvellous'. Following this example, I praise God for the way I am made. My difficulties lead me to seek God with my whole heart, and in seeking God, I have developed a deep relationship with my creator.

God's kingdom is diverse, and we are all members of the body of Christ. Our limitations do not stop God from working in and through us.

So let's celebrate and rejoice in the way we are made, 'for we are [God's] workmanship, created in Christ Jesus unto good works, which God hath before ordained that we should walk in them' (Ephesians 2:10). No matter what challenges we face, we do not have to be ashamed. We can joyfully be who God created us to be.

Prayer: *Dear God, thank you for your love. Thank you for working in and through us no matter our challenges or abilities. Amen*

Thought for the day: I am beautiful because God created me.

Natalie Bernard (North Carolina, USA)

Our focus

Read Matthew 14:22–33

Jesus said, 'Come.' Then Peter got out of the boat and was walking on the water towards Jesus. But when Peter saw the strong wind, he became frightened. As he began to sink, he shouted, 'Lord, rescue me!'
Matthew 14:29–30 (CEB)

The story from today's scripture reading emphasises the importance of consistently focusing on the word of God. In this story, when Peter focused on Jesus – the Word made flesh – he remained above the rough waters. Peter ran into trouble as soon as he shifted his focus from Jesus to the angry waves around him. One moment he was defying the laws of nature; the next he became subject to them and began to sink. A change of perspective changed everything for him.

Like Peter, when we remain focused on God, we can rise above our circumstances. When we focus on our trouble instead of the promises of God, we begin to sink. With faith we can trust in the word of God to grant us peace in our hearts and minds.

Prayer: *Faithful God, thank you for being with us in every circumstance. May we keep our focus on you always. Amen*

Thought for the day: When I focus on God, I can weather any storm.

Nelson Nwosu (Anambra, Nigeria)

The path

Read Proverbs 4:10–19

Direct me in the path of your commands, for there I find delight.
Psalm 119:35 (NIV)

A well-worn path runs along the perimeter of the field behind my house. This path has been made by the countless steps I've taken on its three-mile track. I've walked this path almost every day over the past 15 years. My daily walks serve two purposes. The movement of my body improves my physical health, and my spiritual fitness improves as I meditate, pray and sense God's presence in nature.

I know my path so well that I am able to judge my location just by seeing certain trees, rocks and rain-washed gullies. I usually stay on the path, but when I deviate, I sometimes discover something surprising and unsettling, like a well-camouflaged rattlesnake.

The path behind my house reminds me of the one God has laid out for me. As I walk along God's path, I come to know God's unconditional love, peace and guidance. When I stray, I encounter conflict and chaos. Daily practices like reading scripture, praying and listening for God's response keep me walking along the path. My faith grows stronger with each step I take. I hope my spiritual path becomes as well-worn as the path in my pasture.

Prayer: *Father God, thank you for preparing a path for us that leads to an intimate relationship with you. Help us to stay on that path. In Jesus' name we pray. Amen*

Thought for the day: When I walk with God, I know love and peace.

Lu Fullilove (Texas, USA)

Safe with God

Read Psalm 121

The peace of God that exceeds all understanding will keep your hearts and minds safe in Christ Jesus.
Philippians 4:7 (CEB)

Ever since my teenage years, Psalm 121 has been important to me. At boarding school it was read to us on the last morning of each term. The final verse was especially meaningful: 'The Lord will keep your going out and your coming in' (v. 8, NRSV). Because they were associated with the excitement of going home, those words came to have happy connotations for me.

Psalm 121 was also the psalm my husband and I chose for our wedding service a few years later. Such joyous, reassuring words as we set out into our new life together! God's promise 'The Lord is your keeper' steadied us many times over the years that followed, particularly when we lived in a remote area overseas.

Now I am a senior citizen. My husband and one son have already gone ahead of me to be with the Lord, and I am finding Psalm 121 more valuable than ever. Sometimes a challenge seems too big for me to handle now, but then I hear God's gentle reminder, 'I will keep your heart safe,' and my anxiety is eased. God has kept me through the years – and always will.

Prayer: *Dear Lord, we entrust ourselves to you. Whatever happens, thank you for keeping us safe in your presence. Amen*

Thought for the day: God promises to be with me always.

Elaine M. Brown (Scotland, United Kingdom)

God's timing

Read Psalm 31:14–24

There is a proper time and procedure for every matter, though a person may be weighed down by misery.
Ecclesiastes 8:6 (NIV)

As an avid gamer, many of my favourites are 2D side-scrolling platformers. A well-crafted game of this type can provide a player with an exhilarating feeling of unstoppable momentum as they run and jump towards the end of each level. Proper timing and reflexes are essential as a single missed jump can send the player's character hurtling towards their doom.

While playing a game like this the other day, I suddenly found myself thinking that the need for constant forward progress says a lot about our society. It seems that we are always in a rush to get somewhere or meet some goal. We're told by society and media that if we aren't hustling, we're wasting our time and being passed up by others.

Fortunately, God does not measure time and progress in the same way we do. God is the past, present and future, and while we abide in God our time is not wasted even if the world seemingly passes us by. God's plans for us will be fulfilled.

Prayer: *Dear Lord, help us not to rely on our own perception of time but trust in your divine timing in fulfilling your promises to us. Amen*

Thought for the day: God is faithful in fulfilling promises.

Patrick Castleberry (Mississippi, USA)

Broken and loved

Read Isaiah 43:1–7

The Lord appeared to [Israel] from a distance: I have loved you with a love that lasts forever. And so with unfailing love, I have drawn you to myself.
Jeremiah 31:3 (CEB)

I had been noticing the condition of my mother-in-law's coffee cup for months. The colours had worn, the gold rim had dulled, and now it even had a chip at the edge. I decided that she needed a new mug. So I went to the store, made my selection, then presented it to her. My mother-in-law opened the box and thanked me, but then she placed the mug on her top shelf and poured coffee into her old cup. When I told her I thought it might be time to replace her worn cup, she said, 'Thank you again, but this one is my favourite. My fingers fit the handle perfectly, the edge fits my lips and this cup holds just the right amount of coffee.' The cup's appearance didn't matter to her; it was her special cup and perfect for her.

I believe this is how God sees us. It doesn't matter to God that we have been worn down by our choices, that sometimes our faith fades or even that sin may have chipped away at us. Regardless of our earthly short-comings, we are special to God and God loves us all the same. We are, indeed, precious in God's eyes.

Prayer: *Dear heavenly Provider, thank you for your unwavering, unconditional love. May we live lives worthy of such a gift. Amen*

Thought for the day: Regardless of my imperfections, God loves me.

Monica A. Andermann (New York, USA)

Important lessons

Read Proverbs 1:1–7

Because the Teacher was wise, he constantly taught the people knowledge. He listened and investigated. He composed many proverbs.
Ecclesiastes 12:9 (CEB)

When I was in the eighth grade at school, I took scripture lessons on a weekly basis. The lessons were about stories from the Holy Bible. My scripture teacher asked us to learn by heart the names and order of the books of the Bible and then asked us to recite them in class. Taking these scripture lessons during my preteen period was helpful in my character formation. The lessons strengthened me spiritually and helped me become a more disciplined person.

Now, as an adult, I read the Bible in the early morning during my daily devotional time. When I search for a scripture reading, the memory of the names and order of the books makes it easy for me to find the specific chapter and its verses. When I search for a reading, I remember my thoughtful teacher whose lessons prepared me for the struggles I would face in my life. I am grateful for this grace-filled preparation, which set me out on my journey of faith.

Prayer: *Gracious God, thank you for the people who have prepared us for our spiritual journey. In Jesus' name we pray, 'Our Father in heaven, hallowed be your name, your kingdom come, your will be done, on earth as it is in heaven. Give us today our daily bread. And forgive us our debts, as we also have forgiven our debtors. And lead us not into temptation, but deliver us from the evil one' (Matthew 6:9–13, NIV). Amen*

Thought for the day: Who has helped me on my spiritual journey?

Tun Thwin (Quebec, Canada)

Shepherd the flock

Read 1 Peter 5:1–4

Like shepherds, tend the flock of God among you. Watch over it.
1 Peter 5:2 (CEB)

I was married to an alcoholic who was abusive. Many days I dreaded what might happen when I arrived home from work. During the hardest nights, I would lie awake worrying that he might hurt me while I slept. The police and the courts got involved, and ultimately the marriage ended.

I felt ashamed and discouraged about my marriage and the course of events. I was surprised to find certain friends and family members undependable. It seemed that they were ashamed too. I felt alone – except for God. I prayed continually and could sense that God was guiding me.

Then two older members of my church helped me understand more clearly God's all-encompassing love for me. I expected to be berated and rejected, but instead they surprised me with grace. They met me with keen understanding, guidance and compassion that I had not experienced before.

Now, many years later, I rejoice as I remember this man and woman and how God used them to shepherd me through a very difficult time. My hope is that I may honour God by being the same kind of helper to others.

Prayer: *Gracious and loving God, thank you for never leaving us. Please guide us to those who need our understanding and compassion. Amen*

Thought for the day: God's love for me is all-encompassing.

Carrie Knight Kitzmiller (Texas, USA)

Source of strength

Read Romans 8:18–30

For in hope we were saved. Now hope that is seen is not hope, for who hopes for what one already sees? But if we hope for what we do not see, we wait for it with patience.
Romans 8:24–25 (NRSV)

Watching the eight o'clock television programme one morning made me realise that the clock in our house had stopped. I shook and tapped the clock several times in an attempt to coax it back into action, but it didn't work. When I examined the clock more thoroughly, I found that the battery was loose. No wonder! Without a source of energy, no electronic object will function as it should, regardless of how sophisticated it may be.

This made me think about the times I try to rely only on my own abilities without turning to God for help. But this way of living just makes me fall into deeper difficulties. No matter how mature or independent I think I am, without wisdom and strength from God, my life will be incomplete.

Deciding to follow God wholeheartedly also means entrusting our lives to God. We don't rely on our own greatness anymore. Instead we respond according to the perspective we receive from God's word.

Prayer: *Source of strength, help us to surrender our lives to your care. We pray in the name of Jesus. Amen*

Thought for the day: What is preventing me from relying on God's strength today?

Nike (Riau Islands, Indonesia)

A meagre offering

Read John 6:1–14

[Jesus] said to Philip, 'Where shall we buy bread for these people to eat?' He asked this only to test him, for he already had in mind what he was going to do.
John 6:5–6 (NIV)

Many years ago, I assisted a local church with a children's musical that told the story of the feeding of the 5,000. We used some stage tricks to make this miracle come to life for the audience. But Jesus didn't need stage tricks!

A young boy who had five loaves of bread and two fish offered his meal, meagre as it was for such a large crowd. In the hands of the Son of God, it fed the entire crowd, with twelve baskets of food left over. Jesus transformed that boy's offering into something much greater! The people immediately recognised Jesus as a prophet.

It is easy to overlook the deep concern that Jesus had for the welfare of his listeners in this story. Jesus knows our needs and through God's power provides for us. Even in the midst of the seemingly impossible, Jesus cares and provides.

God calls us to be Christ's hands and feet to transform the world. What can we offer that Jesus can transform? A meal? A hospital visit? A telephone call? A few hours of volunteer service? When we offer what we have, we can trust Jesus to transform it into a gift from God.

Prayer: *Dear God, thank you for the miracles described in the Bible. Help us to offer what we have, trusting that you will continue to work miracles in the world. In Jesus' name we pray. Amen*

Thought for the day: Jesus can transform the gifts I offer in his name.

Eugenia French Shaver (Texas, USA)

Always ready

Read Luke 8:22–25
'Who is this? He commands even the winds and the water, and they obey him.'
Luke 8:25 (NIV)

Growing up in the southwestern United States, we knew that we would have to deal with severe weather from time to time. It could be in the form of drought or a fierce thunderstorm. Sometimes the storms would produce a tornado. One minute you could be standing in the middle of a clear and sunny day, then all of a sudden a dangerous storm would appear.

Something similar happened one day when Jesus and his disciples were in a boat on a calm day crossing over to the other side of a lake. A terrible storm arose, so fierce that everyone feared for their lives. While all of this was happening, Jesus was asleep. The others called to him to wake up. They believed that Jesus would be able to do something to help them. Jesus heard their cry, got up, spoke to the storm and the winds and raging waves became still.

Jesus always anticipated the needs of those he knew needed his help. And Jesus did in fact have the power to calm that storm. Jesus wants us to know that no matter what storms arise in our lives, if we trust him and do not lose faith, he will bring us calm and peace – even in the middle of the storm.

Prayer: *Almighty God, when the storms of life are raging in our lives, stand by us. We know that you have the power to bring calm and safety. In the name of Jesus, we pray. Amen*

Thought for the day: Jesus anticipates my needs and will help me through any storm.

Anthony Sims (Texas, USA)

Intercessory prayers

Read John 17:20–26

I urge, then, first of all, that petitions, prayers, intercession and thanksgiving be made for all people… This is good, and pleases God our Saviour, who wants all people to be saved and to come to a knowledge of the truth.
1 Timothy 2:1, 3–4 (NIV)

The globe in my office shows continents, countries and names of cities around the world. Each day, I spin the globe gently. After a moment or two, I place my finger on the globe to stop the spinning. Then I pray for the people and current situation of the country where my finger is resting.

This practice has great meaning for me. It reminds me that intercessory prayer knows no boundaries. I pray to God for the salvation, spiritual renewal and well-being of the people in the cities and countries whose names I barely know. It is my sincere belief that prayers offered to God from a humble heart extend far beyond this small Caribbean island where I live.

Praying for nations across the globe can transform societies, families and individuals whose faces I can only imagine. John 17 describes Jesus' example of intercession for the people: 'I pray for them' (v. 9). This is a simple yet powerful statement. If Jesus took time to pray for his followers and others, we can do the same.

Prayer: *God of all nations, thank you for your Son who taught us to pray. May we remain faithful in following his example to pray for one another. Amen*

Thought for the day: Intercessory prayers bring us together.

Julianis Báez Pichardo (Dominican Republic)

In the eye of the storm

Read Exodus 19:16–25

*On the morning of the third day there was thunder and lightning,
with a thick cloud over the mountain, and a very loud trumpet blast.
Everyone in the camp trembled.*
Exodus 19:16 (NIV)

My brother died on a June afternoon. That evening as a major storm
rolled in, I felt drawn outside. Wind whipped at my tear-streaked cheeks
and blew my hair in every direction. Shades of grey, blue and orange
streaked the sky. I looked heavenward and saw a flash of lightning and
heard the powerful thunder. I stood outside until pelting rain drove me
back inside. I was filled with unbearable grief. I wanted and needed my
brother. But I knew that through this awe-inspiring display, God was
saying, 'Your brother, whom I love, is here with me.'

In the months following my brother's death, I've read my Bible and
prayed. God directed me to Exodus 19, where the Lord met Moses on
Mount Sinai. The scripture took on a new meaning for me as I read of
thunder, lightning, thick clouds and the quaking mountain announcing
God's presence. I was reminded of the display I witnessed the day my
brother died. God called to me through nature, and I was in God's presence during the storm. God grieved with me and offered comfort and love
for the journey ahead. And God has stayed with me since.

Prayer: *Dear heavenly Father, help us notice the signs that you are
here with us during all the storms of life. Amen*

Thought for the day: I will look for God's presence all around
me today.

Lea Anne Foster (Virginia, USA)

A new wardrobe

Read Luke 24:44–49

'Stay in the city until you have been clothed with power from on high.'
Luke 24:49 (NIV)

I recently had a sort out of my wardrobe, going through every item and sorting them into four piles: keep, chuck, charity shop, recycle. It was amazing how many items I had kept that didn't fit me, suit me or were not fit for purpose any more. Some items were classics that would never date, but some were simply 'no longer me'.

I realised that at times I still 'wear' things from when I was younger that don't fit who I am now – perhaps a 'shawl of shame' of things people have said about me that I have never managed to get rid of. Sometimes when we are younger we don't have much choice about what we wear. But when we accept Jesus into our lives he can give our wardrobe an overhaul – new clothes to reflect how he sees us and who he says we are.

The verse today reminds us that to be clothed with power from on high is the Holy Spirit living within each of us, empowering us, making us more like Christ. Sometimes it can seem particularly challenging to change or believe something different about ourselves, but we know that we are not alone. The Holy Spirit in us can do it, helping us to be the person God always created us to be.

Prayer: *Dear Father, thank you for speaking new truths over us. Help us to believe them, whatever else has been said about me. Amen*

Thought for the day: I am a new creation: the old has gone, the new has come.

Caroline Mansell (England, United Kingdom)

Searching for the Lord

Read Matthew 7:7–11

You will seek the Lord your God, and you will find him if you search after him with all your heart and soul.
Deuteronomy 4:29 (NRSV)

Growing up in a Christian family, I attended church regularly; I knew about the Bible, salvation and Christian teachings. Still, I felt that I didn't know God; I just understood the faith like anything else I learned in school. If someone asked me if I was 'born again', I would say yes, but I really could not explain how.

Once when I was depressed and longing for God, I heard a testimony from a pastor. He said that he found God when he began searching for God's Holy Spirit. At that time, I prayed to God; I wanted to know God and to have a relationship with God. Each day I prayed for God's Holy Spirit to fill me, and I talked to God in my heart constantly. After three days, I began to feel a sense of peace.

Now when I read the Bible, it is not the same as before. The Holy Spirit helps me understand its meaning. I enjoy being in God's presence. I used to be a shy person, but God has helped me become braver and speak out about God's greatness. I want to encourage others who are not sure about their faith to keep praying for God's Holy Spirit to fill them. When we search with all our heart, we will find God.

Prayer: *Dear God, give us a heart that hungers for you. Fill us with your Holy Spirit. Amen*

Thought for the day: The Holy Spirit connects me to God and fills me with peace.

Lairam Lian Thang (Yangon, Burma)

Time with God

Read Philippians 4:4–7

'Be still, and know that I am God; I will be exalted among the nations, I will be exalted in the earth.'
Psalm 46:10 (NIV)

For many years I thought my quiet time with God required at least an hour. And for years I did my very best to make that hour of quiet time happen every day. But suddenly my life seemed busier than ever and much more complicated. So at the very time I needed to be at prayer, I was dismissing it because I did not feel I had that hour to spare.

Recently I came to realise how wrong I was! If my calendar was full to overflowing, a few moments alone with God were much better than none at all. Those few quiet moments changed my whole outlook on a busy day. The quiet solitude not only allowed God to speak to me but also allowed me to listen to God, if only for a few moments.

I embrace those precious hours as often as possible and rest humbly before God in gratitude and praise. I do my best to make those times happen. But when they don't, a few precious moments in the presence of God can be rich nourishment to my soul on a busy day.

Prayer: *Dear God, help us to make the most of every moment with you. Remind us to put you first, regardless of our daily schedule. In Jesus' name. Amen*

Thought for the day: Moments spent with God can make a big difference in my day.

Belinda Jo 'B.J.' Mathias (Mississippi, USA)

Centred on God

Read Ephesians 4:1–6

'A new command I give to you: love one another. As I have loved you, so you must love one another. By this everyone will know that you are my disciples, if you love one another.'
John 13:34–35 (NIV)

I have a friend who is my neighbour, a member of the church I attend and a fellow follower of Christ. We get together about once a week to talk and enjoy each other's company. One major difference between us is that we each belong to a different political party. We have agreed to put our politics aside and keep our conversation centred on other matters. But this is not easy to do. One of us lets something slip, the other retorts, and we have a disagreement.

These discussions become self-defeating exercises since we both want the same things for our country. Because of our different life experiences and different ways of thinking, we have different opinions on which party offers the best solutions. We cannot prove which of us is correct, and it becomes one opinion against another.

We agree that we both belong to the kingdom of God. God requires our accepting one another in love, making 'every effort to keep the unity of the Spirit through the bond of peace'. We have agreed not to let lesser concerns come between us but to keep our beliefs, hearts and minds centred on serving God.

Prayer: *Heavenly Father, help us to show people how much you and your kingdom mean to us by sharing the joy we receive from serving you. Amen*

Thought for the day: My ultimate loyalty is to God.

Paul Grafton (Florida, USA)

Snowdrops

Read Song of Solomon 2:8–13

Flowers appear on the earth; the season of singing has come, the cooing of doves is heard in our land.
Song of Solomon 2:12 (NIV)

It felt like winter had lasted all year. I was tired of salting the sidewalk, drying out wet boots and scraping the car windows. My mood reflected the dark, short days. I needed a change, a sign of hope.

As I trudged up the icy walkway to my front door, I noticed a tiny speck of green. It was tucked up against the side of the house where the snow had melted from the warmth of the foundation. There, growing out of the moist earth, was the tiny tip of a snowdrop – a white flower that signals the coming of spring. Today's verse from Song of Solomon rang through my head like a melody. This was my sign of hope. Just as God had promised, new life was returning.

Although it wasn't a full-blown vision of spring, it was a start. I was reminded that God will do the same thing in me if I am open to it. God provides all that we need for seeds of faith planted years ago to take root in our lives. At the proper time they will grow.

Prayer: *Loving God, help us to remember the promises you've planted in our hearts. We trust in you as our true foundation. Amen*

Thought for the day: God provides the support I need to grow in faith.

Allison Lynn (Ontario, Canada)

Singing for Ezra

Read 2 Corinthians 9:6–15

Whatever you do, work at it with all your heart, as working for the Lord, not for human masters, since you know that you will receive an inheritance from the Lord as a reward.
Colossians 3:23–24 (NIV)

When Ezra came to our church, he and I struck up a friendship that led to many conversations and eventually a visit to his country home. But his health failed, and soon he was in our local veteran's hospital and nearing death.

One day I took my guitar and songbook to his bedside and sang hymns to him as he drifted in and out of a groggy state of mind. He would open his eyes and sing along with me and then close his eyes and rest with a smile on his face. I played and sang quietly, not wanting to disturb any other patients. But as I reached the end of my visit, a nurse came into the room and said, 'Could you play a little louder? The man across the hall is dying and loves to hear the music.' Wow! How could I have known that the Spirit of God would use my simple act of love for my friend as a blessing to someone else?

Our acts of love and service reverberate beyond our imagination and become instruments through which God blesses others.

Prayer: *O Lord, open our eyes to the needs of those around us. Help us to be your voice and your hands of love. Amen*

Thought for the day: By serving others I am serving God.

Brian A. Wolfe (Pennsylvania, USA)

A diligent listener

Read Luke 10:38–42

Let the wise listen and add to their learning, and let the discerning get guidance.
Proverbs 1:5 (NIV)

As my husband and I paddled our kayaks, we spotted fish swimming in the water and alligators sunning on the bank. Soon another kayaker manoeuvred over to us and whispered, 'Look! A manatee!' We marvelled as a manatee swam below us. At that moment, three other kayakers came into view. One shouted, 'I don't see any manatees!' Another shouted back, 'Maybe they are farther down the river. Let's go!' They propelled themselves quickly through the water before we could alert them to the manatee's presence.

As we continued our slow river trek, I thought about those three people. Distracted by their efforts, they did not hear the hushed voices that led others to the manatee. They failed to notice us, still and quiet, gazing into the water. Later I wondered: *How often am I like those kayakers? What acts of service go undone or prayers of intercession go unspoken because I am too distracted or too hurried to attend to the Holy Spirit's nudges?*

There are times when we must make preparations like Martha. Like the three kayakers, we may find cause for forging ahead. However, Jesus values Mary's choice to listen. I hope to follow Mary's example and become a diligent listener – listening with my ears, with my eyes and with my heart.

Prayer: *Dear Father, help us to listen as we study your word, interact with your children and seek your will. In Jesus' name we pray. Amen*

Thought for the day: Today I will be diligent in listening for the Holy Spirit.

Terry J. Burns (Florida, USA)

Flood waters

Read Psalm 29:7–11

The Lord sits enthroned over the flood; the Lord is enthroned as King forever. The Lord gives strength to his people; the Lord blesses his people with peace.
Psalm 29:10–11 (NIV)

When my son was in the neonatal intensive care unit, his health and his ability to breathe independently were out of my control. But so, it seemed, was everything else. My father-in-law was ill, my car wouldn't start, and we had plumbing issues at home. As much as I tried not to worry, I didn't feel hopeful about anything.

Then one morning I read Psalm 29, and verses 10 and 11 resonated with me. The previous verses mention majestic forests, mountains and great trees. They speak to God's power in a way that commands a response of awe. But verse 10 points to flood waters. That's more what my life felt like. Yet David says that God rules over the flood – over the hard, ugly aspects of our lives. Even though I felt overwhelmed, God was not.

On my own, I couldn't think positively any more than I could will my child's lungs to fill with air. In recognising God's power in every aspect of life, I could ask for God's blessing of peace. I didn't have to have a positive outlook; I could acknowledge that life felt difficult. Instead of trying by my own means to be hopeful, I asked God to give me strength and peace, knowing that God rules even in the flood.

Prayer: *Dear God, we know that you are in control, even in difficult circumstances. Bless us with your strength and your peace. Amen*

Thought for the day: I will remember that God rules over even the difficult times in my life.

Ree Pashley (Arusha, Tanzania)

Only forgiveness

Read John 21:15–17
Peter replied, 'Man, I don't know what you're talking about!' Just as he was speaking, the cock crowed.
Luke 22:60 (NIV)

Every day as I climb out of bed, I am troubled with thoughts like these: *Remember when you insulted that person? Remember when you skipped your devotional time? Can't you just try to do something right today?* This spiritual battle rages across my mind most days.

But I take courage from the story of Jesus appearing to his disciples after his resurrection. He had breakfast with them after a miraculous catch of fish, and after breakfast, Jesus asked Peter three times if Peter loved him. Jesus used the repetition to remind Peter of the night when he denied Jesus three times. However, Jesus wasn't condemning or shaming Peter. He was telling Peter, 'Listen, I forgive you! Now go and tell others of my love.'

Peter thought he had failed miserably, but this wasn't the end for him. By accepting Jesus' unending forgiveness, he was able to reach thousands with the same grace that had turned his life around.

I still struggle with keeping my mind fixed on the Lord's redeeming love. Too often I am tempted to focus on my needs and wants instead of on the work of Christ. But God constantly lifts me up from my failures to shape me into a more faithful Christ-follower.

Prayer: *Loving Father, thank you for your forgiveness and for helping us to live the way of Christ. Amen*

Thought for the day: God can use any circumstance to teach me.

Cole Beckloff (South Dakota, USA)

A caring heart

Read 1 Samuel 16:6–13

'The Lord does not look at the things people look at. People look at the outward appearance, but the Lord looks at the heart.'
1 Samuel 16:7 (NIV)

When I arrived at the hospital by ambulance, no beds were available in the emergency room. Instead I was put into a wheelchair and taken to a large room where I would sit all day, waiting for care. Then a biker with tattoos and chains around his neck entered the room and sat down by his elderly mother. I felt uncomfortable and apprehensive at his being there. In the late afternoon, he overheard me saying that I am diabetic and hadn't eaten since 5:00 a.m. He jumped up and said, 'That's terrible! I'll tell the nurse you need some food.' Later he said, 'You look cold. I'm going to get you a blanket.' He returned with a blanket and tucked it around me in my wheelchair. This man had a compassionate and caring heart, and I had misjudged him based on his outward appearance.

In today's scripture reading, Samuel made a similar mistake. God sent him to the home of Jesse to anoint the son that God had chosen to be king. When he saw Eliab, Samuel liked the way he looked and thought he must be the one God had chosen. But God said, 'I haven't selected him. God doesn't look at things like humans do. Humans see only what is visible to the eyes, but the Lord sees into the heart' (1 Samuel 16:7, CEB). I learned a valuable lesson. This Bible story and my experience in the hospital remind me to have compassion for all humanity.

Prayer: *Dear God, forgive us when we misjudge others. Help us to see others as you see them. Amen*

Thought for the day: Today I will look for Christ in every person.

Donna L. Williams (Pennsylvania, USA)

A handful of flour

Read 1 Kings 17:7–16

This is what the Lord, the God of Israel, says: 'The jar of flour will not be used up and the jug of oil will not run dry until the day the Lord sends rain on the land.'
1 Kings 17:14 (NIV)

The Covid-19 pandemic has greatly affected the financial security of my family, and I worry about our future. My worries fill my thoughts, drain my energy and affect my spiritual life. Yet I have tried to do everything in my power to find additional income for us, including taking orders for baked goods.

One afternoon, while I was in my kitchen carefully measuring ingredients for an order of cookies, I made a connection to scripture that I never had before. The widow at Zarephath also understood the experience of careful measuring. All she had was a handful of flour and a little oil – enough for one last loaf of bread for her and her son. When Elijah asked her to give him this last meal, her faith and obedience to God were tested. She trusted God, and God worked a miracle, allowing everyone to be fed.

When we feel trapped by our circumstances and certain that what we have will not be enough, God can work miracles. Today's scripture story strengthens me to continue using what little I have, trusting that with God's help it will be enough to take care of my family.

Prayer: *God who preserves our lives, teach us and guide us every day so that we will continue to feel the miracle of your care. Amen*

Thought for the day: What will I do with the 'flour and oil' I have?

Gloria W. Sinaga (Jakarta, Indonesia)

Staying connected

Read John 15:1–8

'The Advocate, the Holy Spirit, whom the Father will send in my name, will teach you all things and will remind you of everything I have said to you.'

John 14:26 (NIV)

Recently I was leading a Bible study group and we were watching a video together on my laptop. The speaker was talking about the need to stay connected to God by the Holy Spirit. As we watched, I felt that the Lord was saying to me, 'What happens when you run the computer on its batteries?'

The answer was obvious: it will only run for so long, until its battery life is exhausted; it needs to stay connected to the mains to keep working. (In fact, I had moved the table nearer the wall in order to plug the laptop in.) It was such a simple thing, but God was reminding me that I cannot work for him in my own strength. By prayer and Bible study, I need to be connected to the source of power – God himself through the work of the Holy Spirit.

Today's passage speaks of the vine and the branches and the ability to bear fruit that comes from remaining in Christ. Most of us today are more familiar with technology than agriculture, so we may change the metaphor, but it still points to the same truth – we need to ensure we are plugged in to our source of life and power.

Prayer: *Dear Lord, help us always to keep connected to you, our source of life and power. Amen*

Thought for the day: Am I trying to run on my own batteries?

Hilary Hartley (England, United Kingdom)

Unanswerable questions

Read Psalm 62:5–8

Whoever dwells in the shelter of the Most High will rest in the shadow of the Almighty. I will say of the Lord, 'He is my refuge and my fortress, my God, in whom I trust.'
Psalm 91:1–2 (NIV)

On a July morning, two police officers came to our home. With regret they informed us that our 23-year-old son had committed suicide. Deep sorrow broke our hearts. We struggled against such an enormous loss and asked, 'Why did this happen? Why did our son do this to himself?' We asked God, 'Why did you allow this to take place?' We wanted to understand. Though we kept repeating the questions, we found no answers.

When I asked for help, God revealed to me through Psalm 91 what I needed most: to rest in God's presence and trust in God's love and goodness. I knew that this was possible only through a deep and intimate relationship with Jesus. Reading scripture gave me strength to go on. In prayer, I poured out my heart to Jesus. In time, I came to a place of peace, and the tormenting questions lost their power over me.

Most of us have experienced an event in our lives that left us with more questions than answers. In the face of unanswerable questions, Jesus is present to help. When we seek him in scripture, reflect on his love and obey his commandments day by day, we will find rest for our troubled spirit.

Prayer: *Dear God, help us to remember that only you can provide for us a place of needed rest and refuge. Amen*

Thought for the day: God loves hearing my questions.

Cynthia M. Kroll (Oregon, USA)

In community

Read Judges 1:1–10

God sets the lonely in families.
Psalm 68:6 (NIV)

When I was younger, I had this notion that I had to do everything by myself. I believed that asking for help would give glory to others that belonged only to God. However, as I have gotten older, I have realised that God created me and put me in the midst of people – family, friends and community – because I need people.

I have learned that accepting help is a way of acknowledging that I can't do it all by myself. I need God and the help of others around me. Over the years, I have seen God come into my life as a friend's warm hug. God has met my needs through people I did not expect, sometimes even comforting me through the kindness of a stranger. God works in mysterious ways.

In today's scripture reading, Judah asked his brother Simeon for help in the battle against the Canaanites. As they fought side by side, God gave them the victory. God often reaches out to us through family and through community. It's okay to ask for help even as we give help to those around us. When we do, we participate in God's miracles.

Prayer: *Dear Father, thank you for family and for all the people you have used to accomplish your purpose in our lives. Help us to continually trust in you. Amen*

Thought for the day: God reaches out to me through my community.

Toluwalogo Niji-Olawepo (Kwara, Nigeria)

Christmas every day

Read Luke 2:1–7

'Remember, I am with you always, to the end of the age.'
Matthew 28:20 (NRSV)

Every Christmas season, we buy poinsettias to help us celebrate Christ's birthday. Bright red, pure white or variegated blooms add a festive atmosphere wherever they are. Some say the flower represents the star that led the wise men to Bethlehem. For others, the white blooms symbolise purity. This year I have found new meaning in the plant; it is a reminder that Christ is always with us.

Usually after putting away the Christmas decorations, we get back to normal life and forget about our poinsettia. But last Christmas, my family did something different. Instead of neglecting it until it withered away, we placed our poinsettia on our kitchen counter where we see it every day and are reminded of the wonder of Christmas, when Christ came to earth. We water it as needed, and it is still beautiful, even producing new leaves at the end of September.

This plant reminds me of the love that God showed us in sending God's own son to earth. Seeing the still-living poinsettia reminds me that God lives and never leaves us. Indeed, our Lord is with us every day, all year long, even 'to the end of the age'.

Prayer: *Faithful God, thank you for sending Jesus to be with us always, each and every day. Amen*

Thought for the day: How can I share the miracle of Christmas with others today?

Steve Schlesselman (Oklahoma, USA)

Uphill with God

Read Psalm 46

The Lord will keep you from all harm – he will watch over your life.
Psalm 121:7 (NIV)

I need a walk, I thought. *I must have some time outside with God.* Worries were pressing down on me. I live in a valley surrounded by abundant hilly countryside. When I'm facing challenges and my mind needs peace, I love walking up the hills to calm my heart and mind.

In the fresh air that day, my body and mind began to relax. As I trudged uphill, my legs ached, I was thirsty, and I could hear the sound of my breathing and my heart pounding. But determination and necessity pressed me forward. The challenge was worth it because I was away from distractions, and the quietness refreshed me. From the top of the hill, surrounded by beauty, I gained a different perspective. My thoughts slowed down, and in the solitude I was reminded that whatever we face, we are never alone – our loving Father promises to watch over and guide us.

Sometimes we become exhausted when life is tough, especially when stress overwhelms us. Whatever we are going through, God is close by, offering us strength, courage and perseverance. We experience joy and spiritual growth in our uphill walk with God.

Prayer: *Loving Father, thank you for watching over us and guiding us. Give strength to those in need today. In Jesus' name. Amen*

Thought for the day: God is by my side through life's uphill struggles.

Cindy Lee (England, United Kingdom)

The least of these

Read Matthew 25:34–40

'The King will reply, "Truly I tell you, whatever you did for one of the least of these brothers and sisters of mine, you did for me."'
Matthew 25:40 (NIV)

I spend a lot of time with children who have extra needs or are neuro-divergent, both in my personal life and in my work life. I have noticed recently how much joy I get from their company and how rewarding it is when I can help them grow or make them smile. I so often look at them and feel a great sense of love and an awareness of how much each of them brings to the world. As I think on these things, God has been bringing Matthew 25:40 to mind often, showing me that Jesus is there in their smiles and that it gives him great pleasure when I serve them.

Of course, there are many times when it takes sacrifice and hard work serving little ones or those with extra needs. Many of us who are in these caring roles can experience times of isolation. In our culture, we are also often discouraged if we feel our work is not 'important', well-paid or flashy. This passage is an encouragement to those of us who sometimes feel this way. Stay-at-home mums or dads – when you feed your little ones, God sees you and loves it. Carers and nurses – when you get your patients dressed, God sees you and loves it. This passage is an encouragement for anyone who offers practical care in any context and reminds us that the simple, small things are holy and pleasing to God.

Prayer: *Lord, help us to see you in all people. Amen*

Thought for the day: What acts of kindness can I do today?

Amy Turner (England, United Kingdom)

Choose mercy instead

Read 1 Kings 11:1–13

'Why do you look at the speck of sawdust in your brother's eye and pay no attention to the plank in your own eye?'
Matthew 7:3 (NIV)

Reading through the Bible recently, I came across 1 Kings 11 and the account of Solomon's involvement with foreign women who turned his heart to other gods. As I read about Solomon's disobedience, I found myself judging his actions. *How could Solomon turn his back on God? Solomon had built God's temple, and now he was worshipping idols!*

But then the Lord reminded me of my own sin. Like Solomon, I am not exempt from disobeying God and following my own path. I find it often easy for me to condemn the actions of others while ignoring the areas slowly stealing my heart away from God. I have put other things before God, reading my Bible and praying. I had to admit that I too had idols, even if they didn't look like Solomon's.

Judging the actions of others is something Jesus warns us about: 'Do not judge, or you too will be judged' (Matthew 7:1). As there were for Solomon, consequences abound for our disobedience. How thankful I am for God's word, which continually brings me back to reality and back to God's love, forgiveness and grace!

Prayer: *'Our Father in heaven, hallowed be your name, your kingdom come, your will be done, on earth as it is in heaven. Give us today our daily bread. And forgive us our debts, as we also have forgiven our debtors. And lead us not into temptation, but deliver us from the evil one' (Matthew 6:9–13). Amen*

Thought for the day: When I'm tempted to judge, I'll follow Jesus' example and choose mercy.

Teresa Todt (Illinois, USA)

Our salvation

Read Psalm 118:8–16

It is better to take refuge in the Lord than to trust in humans.
Psalm 118:8 (NIV)

When things go wrong, it can feel as if a heavy weight has fallen on our shoulders; in desperation to fix the problem we turn to others for help. When we need to deal with paperwork, repair a car or seek medical help, we know where to turn to get the assistance we need. But what happens when the person who is supposed to help us fails or doesn't have time? We may blame them for our problems, or we may even blame God.

When we seek the help of other people before we seek God's help, we lose sight of the central tenet of our faith: Christ is our salvation. We need to put all our hope in God because God is the ultimate source of our rescue. God knows every part of our lives, understands what we are going through and is ready to move us towards the help we need. When we prioritise our relationship with God, we make room for God to act in our lives. When Christ is first in our lives, we can sense God's presence in every situation.

Prayer: *Dear Lord, thank you for the gift of salvation. Forgive us when we fail to put you first in our lives. Amen*

Thought for the day: Jesus Christ is my salvation and the source of all I need.

Marko Pal'a (Prešov Region, Slovakia)

The gift of prayer

Read 1 Thessalonians 5:12–18
Pray continually.
1 Thessalonians 5:17 (NIV)

Throughout her life my mother prayed diligently. At the top of her prayer list was her family – my father, my sister and me. When she died, what grieved me most was that the one person who prayed for me every single day of my life was gone. My grief made me realise just how important it is to pray continually for others.

So now I have a calendar on my refrigerator that marks the birthdays of people in my life: family, close friends, social media contacts, former work colleagues, church members and college classmates. I make it a point to pray diligently for these extraordinary people during the month of their birthday. I contact those I know well to ask if they have anything specific for which they would like me to pray. Sometimes I get a list, sometimes not. Some people on my calendar have no idea that I am praying for them. But I pray anyway.

Just as my mother's prayers brought comfort to me, I hope others are encouraged to know I am praying for them. But truth be told, the joy is mine – because when I pray for others, I celebrate the unique and wonderful people God created them to be and the blessings they are in my life.

Prayer: *O Lord, thank you for the people you have brought into our lives. Bless them with your presence, and help them to know how much you love them. Amen*

Thought for the day: Praying for others is a gift I give to them and to myself.

Carroll Ellis Cobb (Virginia, USA)

Rereading

Read Psalm 119:12–18
Your word is a lamp for my feet, a light on my path.
Psalm 119:105 (NIV)

I write Christian mystery novels. As soon as I finish a chapter, I edit it. I used to think I only needed to edit my chapters once. I also used to think that once I read through my Bible a couple of times, I didn't need to read it again because I had gotten all there was to get in each passage. I was wrong in both cases. I have learned that with each successive edit I find something I've overlooked.

In a similar way, I have learned that I can read the Bible over and over and not tire of reading the same words. Each time I read a passage again, I find that the stories and my understanding are 'new every morning' (Lamentations 3:23). As I reread a verse, I often find myself saying, 'I never noticed that before.' New insights, new thoughts and new blessings come from the same verses I have read many times before.

So I edit and re-edit my writing, I read and reread my Bible, and I get new meanings and new ideas from both. An inexhaustible source of strength and peace, the Bible offers us new wisdom each day as we read and reread the powerful words.

Prayer: *Dear Lord, help us to understand the importance of scripture, and fill our minds and hearts with a love for it. In Jesus' name. Amen*

Thought for the day: I can trust scripture to offer new insights each day.

Ken Claar (Idaho, USA)

Time with Christ

Read John 1:35–42

'Come,' [Jesus] replied, 'and you will see.' So they went and saw where he was staying, and they spent that day with him.
John 1:39 (NIV)

My job requires me to interact with many people, and that demands a lot of patience. I constantly have to keep in mind that the Lord has called me for this purpose, and therefore it is my responsibility. Because a project I was working on was nearing completion, the workload on a particular day was heavy. I was unable to cope because I was continually faced with questions from others. There was no peace within me, and I was agitated.

During that week, I was reading John 1 where Andrew was looking for the place where Jesus was staying. Jesus' reply to Andrew in John 1:39 challenged me. At the end of my reading time, I paused and asked myself, *What am I searching for?* During this time, the Holy Spirit reminded me that I should stop and rest at the feet of Jesus, so I spent some time in meditation. This quality time I spent with Christ blessed me with calm and renewed my faith. The peace in my mind enabled me to think clearly, and I saw how to address the issues at work. This experience reminded me that when I spend time meditating on God's word, I can find peace that surpasses understanding.

Prayer: *Loving God, amid all our responsibilities, guide us to spend quiet time at your feet to listen to your voice. Amen*

Thought for the day: When I spend time at the feet of Jesus, I am sure to find peace and comfort.

Mihiri de Silva (Sri Lanka)

No kindness too small

Read Acts 2:32–35

Whoever is kind to the poor lends to the Lord and will be repaid in full.
Proverbs 19:17 (NRSV)

One day when I was in line at the grocery store, a woman was looking to see how much money she had. Sadness grew on her face as she saw she did not have enough to cover everything. She ended up having to leave a couple of items behind. As she walked away, the person right behind her told the cashier to put her remaining groceries on his tab. The box boy grabbed the groceries and chased after the woman as she left. A few minutes later she came bounding back into the store, thanking everyone she could find for helping with her purchase. She never found the person who actually bought those last couple of items, but he saw her and had a big smile on his face.

Jesus wants his followers always to look for opportunities to serve, to 'pass his love forward'. For that man the amount of money he spent for the woman's groceries may not have been very much; but to her, it was significant. I don't think there can truly be anything called a 'small kindness'. What we may consider insignificant might move someone from sadness to hope. As Christians we should understand that no matter how small the kindness we exhibit, it can be magnified many times over by God to change someone's life.

Prayer: *Dear Lord, strengthen us to show your love and kindness to everyone we meet. Amen*

Thought for the day: There is no such thing as a small act of kindness.

Wayne Holland (Nevada, USA)

One piece at a time

Read Luke 12:22–34

*Do not worry about tomorrow, for tomorrow will worry about itself.
Each day has enough trouble of its own.*
Matthew 6:34 (NIV)

My husband and I have been working on a jigsaw puzzle. At first it was fun, but the enjoyment wore off when we got to a part of the puzzle where all the pieces were shades of green. Needing help, I joined an online puzzle group and asked for suggestions. The most helpful advice was: 'One piece at a time.' I've taken this advice to heart. With patience and persistence, we will complete the puzzle one piece at a time.

This got me thinking about how God gives us one day at a time. No matter how much we plan for or fret about the future, we only have what God has given us today. In today's reading, Jesus reminds us that being anxious over the future does us no good. We can't add a single hour to our life.

We worry about finances, health, loved ones and relationships. But regardless of what may be disturbing us, it is important to focus on God's loving and almighty power. We can rest in God and fix our eyes on the one who made the world. God has a grand design for creation, and God knows exactly where you and I fit in.

Prayer: *Heavenly Father, help us to trust you even when we can't understand how our circumstances fit into your bigger picture. Amen*

Thought for the day: Today, instead of worrying about my future, I will focus on God.

Elizabeth Erlandson (Nebraska, USA)

When the storms are big

Read Isaiah 41:8–10

Don't fear, because I am with you; don't be afraid, for I am your God.
I will strengthen you, I will surely help you; I will hold you with my
righteous strong hand.
Isaiah 41:10 (CEB)

When I learned I was pregnant, my husband and I were scared. I'd had previous pregnancies end in miscarriage, and just before this I'd had an ectopic pregnancy. Given my history, my doctor immediately prescribed hormone supplements. My husband insisted we get them before we went home. He did not want to take chances.

When we got home, I climbed into bed, scared and in tears. I prayed to God that I would be able to keep this baby. I thought that I would feel better after praying, but nothing had changed. I decided to search for a scripture that would help me overcome my fear. I desperately wanted reassurance from God. That's when I came across Isaiah 41:10. I decided I would read and meditate on that verse daily. I wrote it on sticky notes and put them on my walls, and I made it my phone wallpaper.

In time I started believing what I was reading. I trusted that throughout this pregnancy, God would be with me regardless of the outcome. To exercise my faith, I started buying baby items. By then I had no doubt that I would carry my baby in my arms. I had a smooth pregnancy and gave birth to a healthy baby boy.

Prayer: *Dear God, when we are scared and worried, remind us to turn to you and your promises in scripture. Amen*

Thought for the day: Scripture reminds me that God is with me.

Tumi Mogodi (South Africa)

Why wait?

Read Romans 16:1–15

I commend to you our sister Phoebe, a deacon of the church in Cenchreae.
Romans 16:1 (NIV)

My good friend's health is declining. He has experienced two episodes of heart failure, and another occurrence could end his life. He is a member of a church where I once served as pastor. Knowing I will be asked to pay tribute to him at his funeral, I began to ponder his many admirable qualities. As I was organising my thoughts, I was struck by the incongruity in my thinking. Why was I waiting until my friend's funeral to honour him? It would be far better to express my appreciation now so that he can be encouraged and blessed. So I wrote him a letter and received an appreciative response.

The apostle Paul was not hesitant to express appreciation for his co-labourers in Christ. In the final chapter of his letter to the Romans, he greets no fewer than 28 individuals. He mentions many by name, as well as the contribution they were making to his ministry and the cause of Christ. I'm sure they were heartened by Paul's commendation.

To remain faithful, we need the support of other believers. We all need words of appreciation now, not just accolades after we die. May God's Spirit guide us to someone who needs encouragement today.

Prayer: *Lord God, help us to be encouragers to our friends by showing them your love in our words and actions. Amen*

Thought for the day: Don't put off giving encouragement to someone who needs it now.

Wayne Greenawalt (Illinois, USA)

Hidden hurts

Read Matthew 11:25–30

'Come to me, all you who are weary and are carrying heavy burdens, and I will give you rest.'
Matthew 11:28 (NRSV)

I glanced at my five-year-old daughter just as she touched the tip of a hot glue gun. She silently yanked her finger back, hid her hand in her lap and bent forward in pain. I exclaimed, 'Piper! Are you okay?' I pulled her hand from her lap and saw a large blister on her fingertip.

Piper is independent, tough and always trying to keep up with her three older sisters. As I ran cold water over her finger, I recalled many other instances of Piper hiding her hurts from me: when her skin got pinched in a heavy metal clip, when she took a nasty fall off her bike, when she was being teased at school. It pains my heart to watch Piper hurt alone. I want her to come to me and tell me how she is hurting so I can comfort her and help carry her pain.

Reading Matthew 11:28, I think Jesus feels the same way about us. So why am I reluctant to bring my hurts and burdens to him? Jesus loves us and wants us to tell him our hurts, even though he already sees and knows them. When we come to Jesus, pouring out our weary hearts, he gives us rest.

Prayer: *Loving Lord, help us to bring our hurts and heartaches to you. We thank you for the rest you offer. Amen*

Thought for the day: I will share my burdens with Jesus, who offers me comfort and rest.

Kate Rietema (Michigan, USA)

Community makes a difference

Read Acts 2:42–47

John answered, 'Anyone who has two shirts should share with the one who has none, and anyone who has food should do the same.'
Luke 3:11 (NIV)

One day, a bakery donated five times their regular amount of day-old bread to the donation programme run by the pregnancy centre in our city. It was more than the pregnancy centre needed, and their freezer was too full to store it. To prevent the bread from expiring and going to waste, the leaders of the centre reached out to a large church which had begun a boxed-lunch ministry to feed those who were homeless, fleeing domestic violence or had low incomes. It just so happened that the church programme had forgotten to order bread for that day, and the organisers were delighted to receive this donation.

The workers at the bakery didn't know the needs of the pregnancy centre or the church that day, but God did. And when these two organisations partnered together, they made a difference for many in need. When God prompts us to care for the most vulnerable, God may be working out the details in amazing ways. We can be part of a community of donors working together to make a difference.

Prayer: *God our Provider, thank you for supplying our needs. May we listen as you prompt us to be a part of your community of givers. Amen*

Thought for the day: How is God asking me to care for the most vulnerable in my community today?

Sandi Somers (Alberta, Canada)

Too perfect

Read Romans 12:1–8

Do not be conformed to this age, but be transformed by the renewing of the mind, so that you may discern what is the will of God – what is good and acceptable and perfect.

Romans 12:2 (NRSV)

As we left our hotel while on a recent trip, I noticed several plants in the lobby. They all looked healthy. One in particular, an orchid, had several beautiful blossoms. As I moved closer to the orchid, I reached out to touch a leaf. The leaf felt stiff. Then I noticed the 'soil' in the container was not real. Neither was the plant. Nearer to the door were two other plants I did not recognise. They also had beautiful leaves, but no flowers. I reached out to touch a leaf, assuming it was fake. Then I noticed a brown spot at the end of another leaf. To my surprise it was a real plant! The too-perfect plant was not real. The plant with the blemish was the real one.

The world expects us to have a perfect appearance – perfect skin and the ideal weight, perfect partners and perfect children. Yet pursuing that kind of perfection does not always lead to abundant life.

The Bible reminds us not to live according to the false pretenses of the world, where perfect looks are all too frequently emphasised. Rather we are to focus on the internal gifts and graces, and the renewing of our minds. Jesus loved those with blemishes and those on the margins of society. Likewise we can learn to love ourselves, even though we are imperfect.

Prayer: *O God, help us to love ourselves and to accept our blemishes, realising they are signs of our humanity. In the name of our Saviour, Jesus Christ. Amen*

Thought for the day: I don't have to be perfect for God to love me.

Mike C. Bertoglio (Georgia, USA)

Every opportunity

Read Lamentations 3:19–23

Since it is by God's mercy that we are engaged in this ministry, we do not lose heart.
2 Corinthians 4:1 (NRSV)

Because of my family's economic situation, I had to work for three years before continuing my education. I was excited for the opportunity to go to university.

After finishing my education in law, I had hoped to get a dream job and provide for my family financially. It turns out it's not easy to get a dream job. However, I started working in a religious bookstore, and I have worked there for several months now. Sometimes I feel sad while remembering the dreams and hopes I had when I was in university. I still want a job that allows me to use what I learned there, and I would like to help my family afford my brother's education.

But one day the Holy Spirit spoke to my heart: 'Serving God is a gift and a very special opportunity.' Then I learned to be grateful for every opportunity God has entrusted to me. This special opportunity to work and serve in a religious bookstore comes from God. I don't know about tomorrow, but I'm grateful that today I can serve and work for God.

Prayer: *Dear God, thank you for opportunities to serve and work for you in all that we do. Amen*

Thought for the day: Every chance to serve God is a special opportunity.

Nomi (Indonesia)

A constant reminder

Read Isaiah 40:25–31

Those who hope in the Lord will renew their strength. They will soar on wings like eagles; they will run and not grow weary, they will walk and not be faint.
Isaiah 40:31 (NIV)

When I was in seventh grade, I attended a confirmation class. During one of our lessons, we were challenged to find an image online that reminded us of God. The image I found was an open field, coloured warmly with sunlight. The picture reminded me of all the good times I had at summer church camp. Over the picture was today's quoted scripture.

I decided to use the image as the background on my phone so I could see it throughout my day. It was a nice reminder to look for God in my everyday life. Even during hard times when I had doubts and wondered whether God was really there, the picture and verse continued to remind me that I am a child of God and that my faith will always be a part of me. Now I make sure that at least one of my electronic devices has a lock screen that reminds me of God.

In hard times, it is easy to forget that God has a plan for each one of us. But we can find little ways to remind ourselves that God is near.

Prayer: *Dear God, thank you for drawing near to us. Help us to see your work in our lives. Amen*

Thought for the day: What images remind me that I am a child of God?

Abigail Colbow (Ohio, USA)

From despair to hope

Read Psalm 18:6–19

You turned my wailing into dancing; you removed my sackcloth and clothed me with joy.
Psalm 30:11 (NIV)

I was planning my wedding and excited about starting a new chapter in my life. However, that promise of romance and love never came to fruition – my fiancé suffered a cerebral haemorrhage. Slowly my dream, the joy and the hope in my life faded. Five days later, my fiancé died. My joy was stained with pain, sadness and loneliness. While my mind tried to make sense of it all, my heart was devastated.

My faith, my bedrock, sustained me as I reached out to God with my heart and soul. That faith helped me continue to trust in God's promises. Little by little, renewed strength and a new hope filled my heart. Scripture says that 'those who hope in the Lord will renew their strength. They will soar on wings like eagles' (Isaiah 40:31). I experienced that renewal, trusting in a merciful God to make all things new.

Prayer: *Ever-present God, thank you for sustaining us through grief and pain and for restoring our strength and hope. Amen*

Thought for the day: God's strength is my strength.

Ruth R. Mancilla (Mexico)

Not taken for granted

Read 1 Corinthians 12:14–26

*So we, being many, are one body in Christ, and every one members
one of another.*
Romans 12:5 (KJV)

I tend to take my little toe for granted. But not long ago I had a revelation about that toe's value when it met the leg of my kitchen table. First I heard a crack, and then I felt a pain that forced me to sit down for several minutes until my head cleared. At that moment, no other part of my body mattered; all I could focus on was my toe.

That broken toe affected every other part of my body for weeks. My morning walk changed to a morning hobble to the coffee pot. I traded my regular seat near the front of the church for the one nearest the door. Even getting my shoes on and off was a delicate task. I grew in appreciation for something I often take for granted.

The same is sometimes true in the body of Christ. Maybe there are members of our church or even our family whom we take for granted. Maybe we have overlooked someone's value because we have focused too much on ourselves. But Jesus notices and values each member of his body. After all, Jesus loved each one of us so much that he gave his life for ours.

Prayer: *Father God, help us to see and appreciate others the way Jesus did so that we can show your love to the world. Amen*

Thought for the day: Each person is important in the body of Christ.

Peter Caligiuri (Florida, USA)

Sharing comfort

Read 2 Corinthians 1:3–7

[God] comforts us in all our troubles, so that we can comfort those in any trouble with the comfort we ourselves receive from God.
2 Corinthians 1:4 (NIV)

At a company holiday event, my husband and I arrived early to get seats near the speakers. I wanted to sit close so I could read the speakers' lips because my hearing aids only help so much. Another employee and his wife sat with us. As we introduced ourselves and began to share a little about our lives, I mentioned my hearing impairment. The woman said she was losing her hearing and didn't know what to do next. I didn't have to think about what to say; God gave me the words. I was able to comfort her as God had comforted me when I found out I was going deaf. Since that night, God has given me the words to encourage several other people, even about struggles other than hearing impairments.

A few years later, I was reading 2 Corinthians again. When I came to today's quoted scripture, I became excited. This is what God had been doing in my life! In my struggles I knew that God was there for me because of the promises in God's word. God comforts us so that we can do the same for others. I give thanks for God's comfort and pass it on.

Prayer: *God of compassion, thank you for comforting us. Guide us to comfort others in your name. Amen*

Thought for the day: As God comforts me, I can comfort others.

Sheila Meador (North Carolina, USA)

The whole story

Read Mark 14:27–31, 66–72

Peter remembered that Jesus had said to him, 'Before the cock crows twice, you will deny me three times.' And he broke down and wept.
Mark 14:72 (NRSV)

I recently read the autobiography of a now-departed saint, pastor, author and international speaker. As I read, I was not only inspired by his successes but also impressed by his honesty about his failings. He acknowledged his many mistakes caused by inexperience, pride or arrogance. Reviewing his life, he presented the bad as well as the good.

Peter denied Jesus three times despite having insisted that he would never do that. If I were Peter, I would have made sure that no one wrote down my failings. If I were to write the story of my life, it would be a sanitised, airbrushed masterpiece charting the highs of my association with Jesus and his ministry.

When people are honest about their fears and their failings, we can share in their journeys to a depth that is not possible if they only present the good parts of their lives. Vulnerability, sometimes considered a weakness, is actually a strength. Vulnerability is bravery. Authenticity is connection. I am immensely thankful that the gospel writers captured the embarrassing failings of the disciples as well as their successes. In the gospels we see the arguments, doubts, denials and betrayals. In these accounts, we can see ourselves.

Prayer: *Dear Lord Jesus, forgive our failings. Help us to be brave and vulnerable, strong and authentic, in your service. Amen*

Thought for the day: With God's help I will be vulnerable, sharing my whole self with others.

Andrew Gadd (England, United Kingdom)

A time for everything

Read Ecclesiastes 3:1–8

For everything there is a season and a time for every matter under heaven.
Ecclesiastes 3:1 (NRSV)

I walked around the cornfields near my home. They were empty, barren, void of any life. The wind was the only sound in the low sloping hills. I could relate to those empty fields. I was between jobs, living with my parents, and waiting for someone, anyone, to respond to my job inquiries. I felt like a failure. What had I done by quitting my teaching job and moving back home after three years abroad? Had I misheard God's guiding voice? Had I done the wrong thing? Like the cornfields not yet planted, I was empty.

As I gazed at the field, I remembered a conversation I had with a farmer years ago. We stood at the edge of an empty field like this one, and I asked if he would be planting soon. 'Not yet,' he said. 'We have to wait for the right time, or nothing will grow.' As I stood now alone by the cornfield, I realised that 'empty' was just what I needed to be in that moment. I wanted job offers, but maybe, like the field, I wasn't ready. It wasn't time. Maybe if the offers came too soon, nothing would grow in my life.

It's easy to think of a time of waiting as a time that is wasted. But God, like the farmer, knows there is a time for everything. As the empty field waits for the farmer, we can wait for God's timing.

Prayer: *All-knowing God, give us the strength to wait even when the world seems to tell us we shouldn't. Give us your peace when we can't see the next step to take. Amen*

Thought for the day: I will wait on God's timing.

Rachael Katharine Elliott (Illinois, USA)

Small group questions

Wednesday 3 May

1 What tangible reminders of the importance of prayer, community and supporting one another do you observe in church? How do these physical reminders encourage you?

2 For you, what is meaningful about praying in community? How do your prayers with others differ from your private prayers? Why is this?

3 Describe a time when you witnessed someone acting as a bookend for another person. How did their support change the situation of the person they were assisting?

4 Do you find prayer to be a powerful support? Why or why not? What other forms of support do you find powerful in your Christian community?

5 Who buttresses you with their prayers? Whom do you buttress through prayer? How does having the prayerful support of other believers give you courage and strength?

Wednesday 10 May

1 Are you easily derailed by events from your past? Why or why not? How do you bring your focus back to the present?

2 How do the words in Hebrews 12:1–2 comparing life to running a race encourage you to look ahead rather than look back at negative experiences? What other scripture passages encourage you to keep moving forward?

3 When have you stumbled over something behind you? What caused you to stumble? How did you regain your footing and continue on?

4 How has focusing too much on the past held you back? Does looking back prevent you from deepening your faith and sharing the good news of Christ? Why or why not?

5 What helps you to keep your focus on 'the true pioneer and perfecter of our faith'? Why is focus on Christ so important?

Wednesday 17 May

1 Have you ever felt unequipped for a task God placed before you? Did you accept the task anyway? What was the outcome of the situation?

2 In what ways are you encouraged to know that God can use what is overlooked to make a big impact? How does this change your mindset about what is important?

3 What is in your hand today? Do you consider it small and unworthy, or do you view it as valuable? How will you use what you have to answer God's call to serve?

4 How does God most often show you the value in yourself, your gifts and your abilities? Through scripture, prayer, others, a still small voice? Explain.

5 In what ways is Christian community strengthened when the members embrace their gifts? How might your church look different if each member fully embraced the gifts and talents God has given them?

Wednesday 24 May

1 Are people you meet typically impressed by you and your work, or do they seem unimpressed? How do the responses of others affect your view of yourself and what you do? Why?

2 Have you ever been called to a job or ministry that sounded unglamorous? Did you answer the call? What was your experience, and what did you learn?

3 Besides the story of David, what other Bible stories teach you that every calling from God is important? How do those stories bolster you as you answer your own calling?

4 Do you find it easier to proclaim the power of Christ when you have an elevated platform or when you are doing less 'impressive' work?

5 Recall a time when God empowered you to fight a 'giant'. In what ways does that experience remind you that God will empower you to do whatever God has called you to?

Wednesday 31 May

1 Recalling your spiritual journey, who has played a large part in shaping the direction of your life? What do you imagine your life would be like if that person had not been a part of it?

2 When God brings someone into your life to encourage and guide you, how do you express your gratitude for them and to God? How does gratitude shape your faith?

3 What blessings have others brought into your life recently? How do your prayers and actions change when you are actively aware of the blessings others are bringing to your life?

4 What does it look like for you to have a grateful heart? In what ways do you behave differently when you're feeling such gratitude?

5 Name three ways you intentionally bring blessings to the lives of others. Name three specific blessings you have received from others. How do these reciprocal acts of blessing enrich your life?

Wednesday 7 June

1 When you have to do a task that is outside of your skill set, do you call an expert or do you try to do it on your own? Why? How do your results vary depending on which option you choose?

2 Do you find it easy to turn to God when you need guidance or help with a situation? Why or why not? What helps you lean on God in uncertain times?

3   When you pray for God's will to be made clear to you, how do you discern God's will? After receiving God's guidance, how do you proceed? What do you do when you don't like what you hear?

4   Where or to whom do you most often turn when you need help with an important life matter? Have you ever found guidance through unexpected means? Explain.

5   How does God communicate to you through scripture? How do you embrace that communication from God?

Wednesday 14 June

1   Do you participate in devotional time with your friends? In what ways does spending time with others in this way strengthen your faith and provide you with new insights?

2   Have you ever encountered a Christian teaching only to understand its application at a later time? What caused the message to finally sink in?

3   When someone offends you, do you find it easier to stay angry or to try to see the situation from the other person's perspective? In what ways does your mindset change when you pause and consider God's will for you?

4   Recall a time when God gave you the exact words or company that you needed. How did that experience make you aware of what God was guiding you towards?

5   How do you make time to hear God speaking to you? What spiritual practices and prayers help you to slow down and truly listen? What happens when you do?

Wednesday 21 June

1   Do you strive to be the best and be seen by others as successful? Do you struggle when you experience failure? Why or why not?

2 Are you able to remain hopeful and content even when you are not experiencing success? What helps you to focus on God when you aren't succeeding?

3 How do prayer, scripture and people in your life support you through challenging times? How do they remind you that God loves you no matter how much earthly success you achieve?

4 What is the most meaningful lesson you have learned through failing? How has that lesson impacted your life? How has it affected your relationship with God and others?

5 What scripture passages most clearly remind you that God is good regardless of your situation? How do you cling to those passages when you are overwhelmed?

Wednesday 28 June

1 With whom do you pray regularly? How does that prayer practice draw you closer to God and to your prayer companion? In what ways do your prayer habits differ from your companion's?

2 Do you typically pray aloud or silently? Why? Does this change depending on your situation? Explain.

3 When have you had trouble finding the words to pray? Did you manage to pray anyway, or did you take a break? How do you pray without words?

4 When has someone prayed for you who knew exactly what to say? What is the most meaningful prayer that you can remember someone praying for you?

5 How are you praying for others? How are others praying for you? What difference does this make for you and your ability to live abundantly?

Wednesday 5 July

1 When have you been in a hurry and passed up an opportunity to help someone? How will you respond differently if you are given a second chance to help this person?

2 Have you ever felt compelled to take action when it wasn't convenient to do so? Why do you think you felt this way? How did you respond?

3 Recall a time when you went out of your way to show kindness to someone. What was your motivation? What happened in that situation?

4 How does it encourage you to know that God offers us second chances? What second chance in your life has been the most transformative?

5 Who in scripture best exemplifies a second chance? Why? What can we learn from their response to being given a second chance?

Wednesday 12 July

1 How do you respond to stressful situations? Do you find it easy or difficult to turn to God in times of stress? Why?

2 When have you experienced a much-needed pause in your spiritual journey?

3 Describe a time when scripture provided you with peace and the opportunity to pause. How did your mindset change when you paused?

4 When you experience hardship, how do you make time to pause and be with God? What encourages you to continue praising and trusting God in such times?

5 In what ways does your relationship with God change when you spend more time pausing, reading scripture, praying and worshipping? Why do you think this is?

Wednesday 19 July

1 When have you thought you knew what someone needed, only to learn that you didn't? How did you feel upon realising that what you thought they needed wasn't what they really needed? Why is it sometimes hard to know what others need?

2 What item is special and perfect to you despite its imperfect appearance? What makes this item special? What does it teach you about yourself and God?

3 Do you tend to focus on imperfections or are you able to look past them? Why? How does your answer change in different circumstances?

4 In what ways does knowing that God loves you regardless of your shortcomings and imperfections affect the way you view God? Does it strengthen your faith? How?

5 When you feel unworthy of God's love, what scripture passages and spiritual practices remind you that God's love is unwavering? What reconnects you with God?

Wednesday 26 July

1 Recall a powerful storm you witnessed. Did the storm teach you something new about God? Why do you think being in nature can reveal new spiritual insights?

2 When has God communicated with you in an unexpected way? In what ways did that communication comfort or impact you?

3 Have you ever felt God's presence in a storm, whether real or metaphorical? If so, how did you know God was there? If not, where have you most strongly felt God's presence?

4 Describe a time when a scripture passage took on a new meaning for you. What did you learn or realise? What helped you gain this new understanding?

5　Where do you observe God's presence around you today? What signs show you that God is near?

Wednesday 2 August

1　Have you ever rushed past something you were searching for without realising it? What prevented you from noticing it? Did you ever find what you were looking for?

2　When have you benefitted from quietly observing your surroundings? Why do you think slowing down and paying attention makes such a difference in what we notice?

3　What helps make you more aware of the nudges of the Holy Spirit? How do you attend to those nudges?

4　Do you relate more to Martha or Mary? Why? In what ways is it important for us to emulate both of these women in our daily lives?

5　Who in your life is the best example of quiet listening? What can you learn from them?

Wednesday 9 August

1　Do you prefer to do things by yourself or with help? Why? How does your situation or experience change based on whether you're working alone or with others?

2　Recall a time when you felt God's presence through the comfort and support of others. What was the most meaningful part of that experience for you?

3　Why do you think community is so important for our faith and happiness? Name the three most beneficial things that come from being in community with others.

4　What scripture passages remind you of the value of community and accepting help? In what ways do those passages encourage you as you work to build community in your life?

5   Whom in your community can you ask for help today? To whom in your community can you offer help? How do you think supporting one another brings glory to God?

Wednesday 16 August

1   What task have you found is best accomplished when you repeat it multiple times? Why? What motivates you to do the task again even when you don't feel like it?

2   Do you enjoy rereading scripture passages again and again? Why or why not? How does each new reading give you new understanding?

3   What is the most meaningful insight you have received from a scripture passage? Did you receive this insight on your first time reading it or upon rereading a familiar passage? How did this insight change the way you think of the passage?

4   How are you encouraged to know that the Bible is an inexhaustible source of strength and peace for us? What else serves as an inexhaustible source of strength and peace for you?

5   What spiritual practice or Bible study helps you to find new understanding and insights from familiar Bible passages? In what ways do you continue exploring familiar scripture verses even after you have read them many times?

Wednesday 23 August

1   Have you ever offered a donation without knowing a specific need? What led you to make the donation? What was the outcome, and what did you learn from that situation?

2   Do you find it easy or difficult to listen to God's promptings to care for others? What obstacles get in the way of your caring for others? How do you move past those obstacles to follow God's promptings?

3   Describe a time when you observed God working out the details of a situation in an amazing way. Had you expected the outcome that occurred? Why or why not?

4 When has God supplied your needs in an unexpected way? How did this provision change your situation?

5 What community outreach activities do you participate in? How does your church serve those in need in your community? How do you strive to make a difference for those around you?

Wednesday 30 August

1 Whose autobiography has had a major impact on your life? Why? What did you learn from that person's experiences and reflections?

2 Is it hard for you to acknowledge and admit your mistakes and shortcomings? Why or why not? What happens when you are willing to admit your failings?

3 When have you found that vulnerability and authenticity have deepened your connection with someone else? How did your relationship with this person change?

4 If you were one of the disciples, how would you feel knowing that your good and bad moments were recorded in scripture? Why would you feel this way?

5 Where do you find it easiest to be vulnerable and authentic? Where do you find it most difficult? Who in your life best encourages you to be vulnerable? How do you encourage others to do the same?

Volunteer with BRF

At BRF we believe that volunteers have so much to contribute to our work and ministry as we support churches in their mission. We offer numerous opportunities, including the role of local church champion, whereby a volunteer shares the work of BRF with their local church.

Offering such a wealth of ministries for all ages, we are well placed to support churches in a way that is suitable for them and their context. Our volunteers working with church leadership are able to make a difference to the lives of others.

Our team of volunteers includes people from a variety of ages, denominations and backgrounds, each with varying skills. Some have a particular BRF ministry of interest while others are connected across all ministries.

The role is flexible to fit with each person's availability and varies in each setting. Some share information via their church notice sheet or have contact with specific individuals, such as children's or youth leaders or those working with older people. Others have contacts in their Churches Together network or denominational structures. Being well supported by BRF offers an opportunity to feel connected, as well as getting to know others in a similar role.

Angela in Wiltshire volunteered with the encouragement of her rector to encourage individuals and groups to get closer to God through regular study by highlighting the various BRF resources and updates in the parish newsletter.

Catriona Foster, one of BRF's volunteers, says:

I would sum up my volunteering with BRF as a rewarding and inspiring privilege. Not only is volunteering rewarding and enjoyable but recent research has shown that well-being is significantly improved when people are meeting and helping others and feel valued.

As volunteer Martyn Payne so helpfully expresses:

It is when we reach out to help others that we are most helped. This is the surprising equation of giving and receiving that lies at the heart of our faith in God.

If you or someone you know would be interested in joining the team, please contact **jane.butcher@brf.org.uk**

Become a Friend of BRF
and give regularly to support our ministry

We help people of all ages to grow in faith

We encourage and support individual Christians and churches as they
serve and resource the changing spiritual needs of communities today.

Through **Anna Chaplaincy**
we're enabling churches to provide
spiritual care to older people

Through **Living Faith**
we're nurturing faith and resourcing
lifelong discipleship

Through **Messy Church**
we're helping churches to reach out
to families

Through **Parenting for Faith**
we're supporting parents as they raise
their children in the Christian faith

Our ministry is only possible because of the generous support of
individuals, churches, trusts and gifts in wills.

As we look to the future and make plans, **regular donations make a huge
difference** in ensuring we can both start and finish projects well.

By becoming a Friend of BRF and giving regularly to our ministry you are
partnering with us in the gospel and helping change lives.

How your gift makes a difference

£2 a month — Helps us to give away **Living Faith** resources via food banks and chaplaincy services

£10 a month — Helps us to support parents and churches running the **Parenting for Faith** course

£5 a month — Helps us to support **Messy Church** volunteers and grow the wider network

£20 a month — Helps us to develop the reach of **Anna Chaplaincy** and improve spiritual care for older people

How to become a Friend of BRF

Online – set up a Direct Debit donation at **brf.org.uk/donate** or find out how to set up a Standing Order at **brf.org.uk/friends**

By post – complete and return the tear-off form opposite to 'Freepost BRF' (*no other address or stamp is needed*)

If you have any questions, or if you want to change your regular donation or stop giving in the future, do get in touch.

Contact the fundraising team

Email: giving@brf.org.uk

Tel: 01235 462305

Post: Fundraising team, BRF, 15 The Chambers, Vineyard, Abingdon OX14 3FE

Registered with FUNDRAISING REGULATOR

Bible Reading Fellowship (BRF) is a charity (233280) and company limited by guarantee (301324), registered in England and Wales

SHARING OUR VISION – MAKING A GIFT

I would like to make a donation to support BRF.
Please use my gift for:

☐ Where the need is greatest ☐ Anna Chaplaincy ☐ Living Faith

☐ Messy Church ☐ Parenting for Faith

Title	First name/initials	Surname

Address

	Postcode

Email

Telephone

Signature	Date

Our ministry is only possible because of the generous support of individuals, churches, trusts and gifts in wills.

Please treat as Gift Aid donations all qualifying gifts of money made

giftaid it

☐ today, ☐ in the past four years, ☐ and in the future.

I am a UK taxpayer and understand that if I pay less Income Tax and/or Capital Gains Tax in the current tax year than the amount of Gift Aid claimed on all my donations, it is my responsibility to pay any difference.

☐ My donation does not qualify for Gift Aid.

Please notify BRF if you want to cancel this Gift Aid declaration, change your name or home address, or no longer pay sufficient tax on your income and/or capital gains.

You can also give online at **brf.org.uk/donate**, which reduces our administration costs, making your donation go further.

Please complete other side of form ➲

SHARING OUR VISION – MAKING A GIFT

Please accept my gift of:

☐ £2 ☐ £5 ☐ £10 ☐ £20 Other £ [_____]

by (*delete as appropriate*):

☐ Cheque/Charity Voucher payable to 'BRF'

☐ MasterCard/Visa/Debit card/Charity card

Name on card

Card no. [____] [____] [____] [____]

Expires end [M M] [Y Y] Security code [___] Last 3 digits on the reverse of the card

Signature   Date

☐ I would like to leave a gift to BRF in my will.
Please send me further information.

For help or advice regarding making a gift, please contact our fundraising team +44 (0)1865 462305

Your privacy

We will use your personal data to process this transaction. From time to time we may send you information about the work of BRF that we think may be of interest to you. Our privacy policy is available at **brf.org.uk/privacy**. Please contact us if you wish to discuss your mailing preferences.

Registered with

FUNDRAISING
REGULATOR

↻ Please complete other side of form

Please return this form to 'Freepost BRF'
No other address information or stamp is needed

Bible Reading Fellowship is a charity (233280) and company limited by guarantee (301324), registered in England and Wales

UR0223

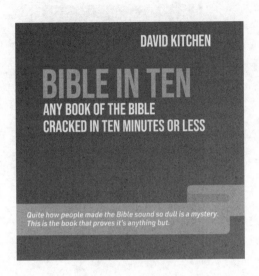

DAVID KITCHEN

BIBLE IN TEN
ANY BOOK OF THE BIBLE CRACKED IN TEN MINUTES OR LESS

*Quite how people made the Bible sound so dull is a mystery.
This is the book that proves it's anything but.*

Bible in Ten is for everyone who wants to be connected with all that is unexpected, beautiful and astonishing in the Bible. It tells the stories of success and failure, suffering and hope, home and exile, and a love that is stronger than death. Here are 67 short, sharp snapshots covering every corner of a book that people sometimes don't know quite as well as they think they do. It's a way into a volume that is often on the shelves but far less frequently taken off them.

Bible in Ten
Any book of the Bible cracked in ten minutes or less
David Kitchen
978 1 80039 151 2 £12.99
brfonline.org.uk

God deeply cares for those of us who are broken and hurt. And just as he helped his beloved Jerusalem find healing in her brokenness, he does the same for us. For he cried out seven double imperatives to her in the book of Isaiah – seven steps to restore her to wholeness – and he cries out the same to us. But he doesn't begin by scolding us; instead, he comforts. His first double imperative is, 'Comfort, comfort,' despite what has happened in our lives.

This Crown of Comfort
God's seven calls to women in distress
Eva Leaf
978 1 80039 208 3 £9.99
brfonline.org.uk

How to encourage Bible reading in your church

BRF has been helping individuals connect with the Bible for 100 years. We want to support churches as they seek to encourage church members into regular Bible reading.

Order a Bible reading resources pack

This pack is designed to give your church the tools to publicise our Bible reading notes. It includes:

- Sample Bible reading notes for your congregation to try.
- Publicity resources, including a poster.
- A church magazine feature about Bible reading notes.

The pack is free, but we welcome a £5 donation to cover the cost of postage. If you require a pack to be sent outside the UK or require a specific number of sample Bible reading notes, please contact us for postage costs. More information about what the current pack contains, go to **brfonline.org.uk/pages/bible-reading-resources-pack**.

How to order and find out more
- Email **enquiries@brf.org.uk**
- Telephone BRF on +44 (0)1865 319700 Mon–Fri 9.30–17.00
- Write to us at BRF, 15 The Chambers, Vineyard, Abingdon OX14 3FE.

Keep informed about our latest initiatives

We are continuing to develop resources to help churches encourage people into regular Bible reading, wherever they are on their journey. Join our email list at **brfonline.org.uk/signup** to stay informed about the latest initiatives that your church could benefit from.

Subscriptions

The Upper Room is published in January, May and September.

Individual subscriptions

The subscription rate for orders for 4 or fewer copies includes postage and packing:

The Upper Room annual individual subscription £19.05

Group subscriptions

Orders for 5 copies or more, sent to ONE address, are post free:
The Upper Room annual group subscription £14.85

Please do not send payment with order for a group subscription. We will send an invoice with your first order.

Please note that the annual billing period for group subscriptions runs from 1 May to 30 April.

Copies of the notes may also be obtained from Christian bookshops.

Single copies of *The Upper Room* cost £4.95.

Prices valid until 30 April 2024.

Giant print version

The Upper Room is available in giant print for the visually impaired from:

Torch Trust for the Blind
Torch House
Torch Way
Northampton Road
Market Harborough
LE16 9HL

Tel: +44 (0)1858 438260
torchtrust.org

THE UPPER ROOM: INDIVIDUAL/GIFT SUBSCRIPTION FORM

All our Bible reading notes can be ordered online by visiting brfonline.org.uk/subscriptions

☐ I would like to take out a subscription myself (complete your name and address details once)

☐ I would like to give a gift subscription (please provide both names and addresses)

Title .... First name/initials .... Surname ....

Address ....

.... Postcode ....

Telephone .... Email ....

Gift subscription name ....

Gift subscription address ....

.... Postcode ....

Gift message (20 words max. or include your own gift card):

....

....

Please send *The Upper Room* beginning with the September 2023 / January 2024 / May 2024 issue (*delete as appropriate*):

Annual individual subscription ☐ £19.05

Optional donation* to support the work of BRF £ ....

Total enclosed £ .... (cheques should be made payable to 'BRF')

*Please complete and return the Gift Aid declaration on page 159 to make your donation even more valuable to us.

Method of payment

Please charge my MasterCard / Visa with £ ....

Card no. ☐☐☐☐ ☐☐☐☐ ☐☐☐☐ ☐☐☐☐

Expires end ☐M ☐M ☐Y ☐Y   Security code ☐☐☐   Last 3 digits on the reverse of the card

> **All our Bible reading notes can be ordered online by visiting brfonline.org.uk/subscriptions**

☐ Please send me .... copies of *The Upper Room* September 2023 / January 2024 / May 2024 issue (*delete as appropriate*)

Title .... First name/initials .... Surname ....

Address ....

.... Postcode ....

Telephone .... Email ....

Please do not send payment with this order. We will send an invoice with your first order.

Christian bookshops: All good Christian bookshops stock BRF publications. For your nearest stockist, please contact BRF.

Telephone: The BRF office is open Mon–Fri 9.30–17.00. To place your order, telephone +44 (0)1865 319700.

Online: brfonline.org.uk/group-subscriptions

☐ Please send me a Bible reading resources pack to encourage Bible reading in my church

Please return this form with the appropriate payment to:
BRF, 15 The Chambers, Vineyard, Abingdon OX14 3FE

For terms and cancellation information, please visit **brfonline.org.uk/terms**.

Bible Reading Fellowship is a charity (233280) and company limited by guarantee (301324), registered in England and Wales

UR0223

To order

Online: brfonline.org.uk
Telephone: +44 (0)1865 319700 Mon–Fri 9.30–17.00

Delivery times within the UK are normally 15 working days. Prices are correct at the time of going to press but may change without prior notice.

Title	Price	Qty	Total
Bible in Ten	£12.99		
This Crown of Comfort	£9.99		

POSTAGE AND PACKING CHARGES			
Order value	UK	Europe	Rest of world
Under £7.00	£2.00	Available on request	Available on request
£7.00–£29.99	£3.00		
£30.00 and over	FREE		

Total value of books	
Postage and packing	
Donation*	
Total for this order	

* Please complete the Gift Aid declaration below

Please complete in BLOCK CAPITALS

Title .... First name/initials .... Surname...

Address...

.... Postcode ....

Acc. No. .... Telephone ....

Email ....

Gift Aid Declaration

giftaid it

Please treat as Gift Aid donations all qualifying gifts of money made (*tick all that apply*)
☐ today, ☐ in the past four years, ☐ and in the future **or** ☐ My donation does not qualify for Gift Aid.

I am a UK taxpayer and understand that if I pay less Income Tax and/or Capital Gains Tax in the current tax year than the amount of Gift Aid claimed on all my donations, it is my responsibility to pay any difference.

Please notify BRF if you want to cancel this declaration, change your name or home address, or no longer pay sufficient tax on your income and/or capital gains.

Method of payment

☐ Cheque (made payable to BRF) ☐ MasterCard / Visa

Card no. ☐☐☐☐ ☐☐☐☐ ☐☐☐☐ ☐☐☐☐

Expires end [M][M] [Y][Y] Security code ☐☐☐ Last 3 digits on the reverse of the card

Please return this form to:

BRF, 15 The Chambers, Vineyard, Abingdon OX14 3FE | **enquiries@brf.org.uk**
For terms and cancellation information, please visit **brfonline.org.uk/terms**.

Bible Reading Fellowship (BRF) is a charity (233280) and company limited by guarantee (301324), registered in England and Wales